HAPPY TRAILS

Variations on the Classic Drunkard's Path Pattern

PEPPER CORY

C&T PUBLISHING

Cover Photo: Drunkard's Path, circa 1890. York, Pennsylvania. Collection of the author.

Copyright © 1991 Pepper Cory

Edited by Sayre Van Young
Berkeley, California

Technical information edited by Janet Macik Myers
Fairfield, California

Cover design and pen-and-ink illustrations by Kathryn L. Darnell
East Lansing, Michigan

Photographs by Sharon Risedorph, San Francisco, California, and Mark Eifert, Portland, Oregon

Design, production coordination, typesetting, and electronic illustrations by
Rose Sheifer Graphic Productions
Walnut Creek, California

Mylar is a registered trademark of E. I. duPont de Nemours & Co.
Multi-View Lens is a brand name of Quilter's Rule.

Published by C&T Publishing
P.O. Box 1456
Lafayette, California 94549

ISBN: 0-914881-43-4

Library of Congress Catalog Card Number: 91-53017

Library of Congress Cataloging-in-Publication Data

Cory, Pepper.
    Happy trails : variations on the classic drunkard's path pattern / Pepper Cory.
— 1st ed.
        p.   cm.
    Includes bibliographical references.
    ISBN 0-914881-43-4 : $14.95
    1. Quilting—Patterns.   I. Title.   II. Title: Drunkard's path pattern.
TT835.C6795   1991
746.9' 7—dc20   91-53017
                                                               CIP

First Edition
First Printing
Printed in Hong Kong

CONTENTS

Dedication 4

Acknowledgments 5

A Word to the Reader 6

1. The History of the Drunkard's Path Pattern 7

2. Before You Sew—Templates and Fabrics 10

3. Designing with the Drunkard's Path 18

4. Sewing the Curve 27

5. The No-Curve Drunkard's Path 49

6. Conclusion 54

Pattern Index for Drunkard's Path and Variations 55

Templates 59

Bibliography 63

Resources 64

The Color Section follows page 32.

DEDICATION

This book is dedicated to my grandmother, Jessie Thompson Welty Wetzel. Born in 1893 in what was then Indian Territory (later Oklahoma), she fought her parents for the right to attend college. After obtaining a degree in Latin, she returned to the family ranch in Memphis, Texas, and became engaged to a local rancher.

One day while out riding, she saw an aeroplane land in a neighbor's pasture. Of course she galloped over and introduced herself to the pilot. He was a young Scotsman, Henry Scott Crawford Peddie, who was helping train American pilots for the coming conflict in Europe. So much for the local rancher. Scott and Jessie were soon married, and my father was the only child of that union.

A widow by the time she was twenty-five, Jessie was both a "flapper" and a career woman in the 1920s. When World War II broke out, she hurried to Amarillo, Texas, where aircraft maintenance instructors were desperately needed. She memorized the parts of the airplane engines and spent the remainder of the war teaching young men to be airplane mechanics. On the other hand, Mama Jess (as her grandchildren called her) never learned to drive a car. She maintained a horse was a better ride.

Once, while shopping in New York City, she emerged from a department store to find herself—and several other shoppers—caught in crossfire between a robber and a pursuing policeman. She shoved the woman in front of her to the pavement until the bullets stopped flying. As Jessie calmly dusted herself off, a gawking bystander asked, "Lady, how did you know when to duck?" Mama Jess straightened her stockings as she answered, "Why of course I'd know the sound of gunfire! I'm from Texas!"

A merciless card shark, Jessie had learned to play poker to supplement the family income. During one visit (I was dealing in antique quilts at the time), I was introduced to her poker buddies as "my granddaughter, the one who sells old blankets." Mama Jess was never the milk-and-cookies grandma, but she will always be an inspiration, a classy lady, and a memorable character. Happy trails to you, Mama Jess.

ACKNOWLEDGMENTS

These people are those generous souls who allowed me to photograph their quilts, helped in the quilting of the samples, encouraged me to finish this book, and generally supported the writing of *Happy Trails*. Thank you all.

Norine Antuck
Susan Bengtson
Barbara Brackman
Mary Jo Houston Braun
Suzie Braun
Ada Brower
Cynthia Buettner
Bonnie Bus
Marti Caterino
Ida Copeland
Pat Cox
Kathy Curtis
Mary Jo Dalrymple
Ruth Dukelow
Gregor Gamble
Helen Gamble
Cynthia Griewahn

Rebecca Haarer
Jan Halgrimson
Barbara Oliver Hartman
Gail Hill
Ardis and Robert James
Doris Lucas
Marsha McCloskey
Nancy Myers
Rebecca Mohr
Louise Mueller
Diane Pedersen
Carol Riffe
Darlene Roberts
Carol Schon
Elly Sienkiewicz
Shirley A. Thompson

A WORD TO THE READER

Experienced hand-piecers will probably not be thrown a curve by the Drunkard's Path pattern. On the other hand, newer quilters and those who regularly piece on the sewing machine tend to bypass the Drunkard's Path. Why this avoidance?

Perhaps when an aspiring quiltmaker encounters her first Drunkard's Path quilt, all she can see are those undulating allover curved seams. It *can* be rather overwhelming. Many books, especially older texts, were not particularly encouraging when it came to the Drunkard's Path. They literally scared quilters away with warnings like "only the most experienced needlewoman ought to attempt this pattern." To put it bluntly, the Drunkard's Path has gotten a lot of bad press. I offer the following observations with the hope that they will reassure the reader who wants to learn about the wonderfully meandering Drunkard's Path, and that they will encourage her to try the pattern.

Every Drunkard's Path block is based on a grid of squares formed from two interlocking pieces—a quarter-circle and its wing-shaped remainder. With the help of this book's step-by-step instructions, illustrations, and a little practice, every quiltmaker can learn to piece the Drunkard's Path curve easily.

Once two curved pieces are sewn together, they make a square. And squares are a snap to sew! Keep in mind that all the twists and turns of a Drunkard's Path quilt are made up of individual quarter-circle curves. The Drunkard's Path is pieced one curve at a time.

Your very first Drunkard's Path sample may not be an unqualified success. On reflection, you may find little things wrong with your work. Good. All that means is that you are not yet through with the Drunkard's Path pattern. In your *next* piece, you can make those corrections, and, I guarantee, more good ideas will come with a second effort. With your third try at Drunkard's Path, you'll feel confident enough to show someone else how to do it.

Even after fifteen-plus years of fooling around with the Drunkard's Path, I am still happily experimenting. It's rather like my favorite flower bed. During the winter I graze through the gardening catalogs. In the spring I happily dig in the dirt planting flowers. I fully enjoy my flower bed in the summer, but by fall, I am ready to move the bulbs around, thinking "This time I'll try it a different way." Just as gardening remains an ever-absorbing interest, so I hope the Drunkard's Path pattern takes root in your imagination and brings you many happy hours creating beautiful quilts.

THE HISTORY OF THE DRUNKARD'S PATH PATTERN

The factual history of the Drunkard's Path is rather sketchy. Like the names of quiltmakers of times gone by, the history of patterns has seldom been recorded or dated with certainty. Names of quilt patterns were indigenous to a region, a certain ethnic group, one family, or even an individual.

Some of the information about the Drunkard's Path is anecdotal or speculative. A few bits of quilt lore are attached to some of the pattern's names. The problem in recording Drunkard's Path patterns reminds me of that famous drawing showing either two faces in profile or a vase in silhouette. So the Drunkard's Path assumed different configurations for different quiltmakers. What one quilter perceived as the Drunkard's Path, her neighbor might not recognize at all.

As seen in Figure 1, there are three areas that might be perceived as the Drunkard's Path block. When examining an old Drunkard's Path quilt, what the quilt's maker considered her basic block can be deduced only if the multiples of the arrangement are easily counted or if there are fabric color changes from block to block.

Figure 1.
All three of the shaded areas indicate possible blocks. All have been considered **the** *Drunkard's Path block.*

DRUNKARD'S PATH

WONDER OF THE WORLD

ALSO CALLED DRUNKARD'S PATH

To simplify the process of examining the many versions of the Drunkard's Path pattern, the variations and the names associated with the pattern may be found in the Pattern Index at the back of this book. The Index is a handy visual reference for the blocks mentioned in the text or shown in the color section.

THE DRUNKARD'S PATH IN ENGLAND

The pattern commonly known as the Drunkard's Path first appeared in early nineteenth-century English quilts. The English versions, for the most part, favored symmetrical arrangements of the quarter-circle-in-a-square units. The English names are indicative of what were, in earlier times, common sights in Great Britain. The water wheel of the local grain mill, turning in a stream, found its namesake in Mill Wheel. Horseracing, the most popular sport of nineteenth-century England, was memorialized in Steeplechase. Even the rider's bicolored hat left its emblem in Jockey Cap, the center of the Steeplechase block.

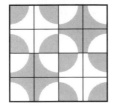

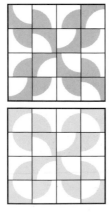

The best-known name for the Drunkard's Path in England was Rob Peter to Pay Paul. Although I had heard that phrase all my life, until I was a quilter, I had never wondered why Peter was robbed to pay Paul. The phrase has come to mean to take money from a fund reserved for the payment of one bill and use that money to pay another bill. It originated in seventeenth-century England when the dean of St. Peter's Cathedral in Winchester refused to sell some of the cathedral's land and turn over the money to St. Paul's Cathedral in London for repairs. It was a hotly debated topic of the day, and since the phrase had a nice alliterative ring to it, to "rob Peter to pay Paul" entered the colloquial speech of residents of both Great Britain and the Colonies.

The name Rob Peter to Pay Paul, probably because it is an older term, has also been applied to other patchwork patterns. It sometimes is used to designate a designing style in which blocks exhibit a color counter-change.

THE MIGRATION OF THE DRUNKARD'S PATH

When the pattern came to the Colonies with settlers of English origin, quiltmakers continued to emulate the symmetrical arrangements of the quarter-circle-in-a-square pattern they had known. But somewhere along the line, American quiltmakers began to devise new arrangements and invent new names for the pattern. Perhaps they wanted to break away from traditional English customs. Or perhaps a new arrangement was the work of some weary quiltmaker who didn't pay attention as she pieced the block.

In some early quilts made in New England, the Drunkard's Path was called the Wanderer in the Wilderness. That name is still popular in Canada. "Modern" versions of the Drunkard's Path began to appear in the late nineteenth century as newspaper columns and books devoted to the needlearts became widely available. Due to the growth of literacy among women in the late nineteenth century, female readers were exposed to more quilt patterns in the daily news than their grandmothers might have encountered in a lifetime. Women readers educated each other as they sent their own patterns to the columns. Quiltmakers formed quilt clubs and joined round robins (groups of quilters who communicated through the mail). Pattern companies, many of them run by women, sprang up to meet the quilting public's demand for patterns. All of these contributed to the interest in and spread of the Drunkard's Path.

THE DRUNKARD'S PATH AMONG THE AMISH AND OTHERS

Although the Drunkard's Path pattern was used by Amish quiltmakers, it was usually called Solomon's Puzzle, Old Maid's Puzzle, or, as one Iowa Amish quiltmaker recorded it, the Old Maid's Dilemma. (See Figure 3.) Curved patterns were never as popular as straight-edged patchwork patterns with the Amish. And perhaps the reference to drink offended Amish sensibilities. It has only been recently, when Amish quiltmakers made quilts to sell to the "English" (non-Amish people), that the Drunkard's Path has been known as such among the Amish.

Precisely because of this association between the quiltmaker and her pattern, the Drunkard's Path pattern has been both in and out of favor at different times. A few quilt historians have suggested that the popularity of the Drunkard's Path pattern in nineteenth-century America reflected the growth of the Temperance movement.

The Temperance movement, composed primarily of women, urged complete abstinence from "all spirits and strong drink." From my research, I cannot agree that the Drunkard's Path was popular with the Temperance ladies. Rather, organizations such as the W.C.T.U. (Women's Christian Temperance Union) favored quilt patterns in which quiltmakers could sign their names and the names of others they could persuade to "take the pledge," i.e., promise not to drink. One such pattern was the Water Goblet. (See Figure 4.)

The unpleasant connotations of the term "the drunkard's path" are not altogether dismissed or forgotten even today. I know a modern quiltmaker (a fourth-generation quilter) who has inherited many family quilts. There is not a Drunkard's Path among the lot. When I asked why, she replied, "My mother and my grandmother told me it was bad luck to piece a Drunkard's Path quilt. The person who slept under a Drunkard's Path quilt might develop a thirst for drink and wander far from home. We still don't make Drunkard's Path quilts in my family." And that was that.

Despite such opinions, the popularity of the Drunkard's Path continued to grow. It was the ideal pattern on which to practice piecing curves. The units within the block invited experimentation. In short, the Drunkard's Path was a challenge. The Drunkard's Path title has come to be viewed, not with alarm, but with amusement and even affection. Every quilter knows the pattern, and most have been meaning to try it "some day." Now's your chance!

Figure 4.
This is one of several quilt patterns the ladies of the Women's Christian Temperance Union made in the hope of persuading drinkers to "take the pledge."

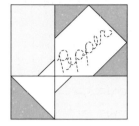

THE WATER GOBLET
(SIGNED)

My grandfather, Henry Scott Crawford Peddie, dressed as a dude cowboy. Texas, c. 1915.

9

BEFORE YOU SEW
TEMPLATES AND FABRICS

P rior to sewing the Drunkard's Path, two topics need to be considered—first, the making of the templates for the patchwork, and second, the buying and preparation of fabrics. These are separate concerns, and only the first—making templates—is an exact science.

TEMPLATES

There are three different kinds of templates—those you buy, those you copy, and those you design yourself. When using commercially made templates, copying template patterns from books and magazines, or even drawing your own, remember to check the accuracy of all measurements. Measure and re-measure the template pieces, making sure they are the exact size you need for your Drunkard's Path project.

My personal preference is to use or make templates with 1) the quarter-inch seam allowances included on them and 2) pinning point holes indicated. I prefer the "quarter-inch-on" style of template since I want to mark pieces as close as possible to each other on the precious fabric! Long ago I decided that marking all my sewing lines was too time-consuming and estimating the quarter-inch seam allowance was a bit sloppy (read dangerous) for me. If I could learn to sew a regular quarter-inch seam, then marking dots to keep me on track should be enough guidance. I still sew dot-to-dot even on fairly simple patterns, and I can piece either by hand or machine on the same quilt because there is no variation in my work.

Commercially Made Templates

Commercially available templates come in either plastic or metal. When using a rotary cutter, a plastic template (acrylic, about ⅛" thick) is the best—not only do they have pinning holes, but they're safer than the thinner metal models. Although you may be accustomed to a large-blade cutter, when cutting around a curved template be sure to use a small-blade cutter. The large blade just will not run smoothly along curves, especially concave ones. Something else to get used to: Since your hand is occupied with guiding the cutter, less downward pressure can be applied. Less pressure means less layers cut at a time. When using the rotary cutter with curved templates, expect to cut only a double layer of fabric at first. When you become more adept (and your wrist is stronger), try adding one more layer of fabric at a time.

Making Your Own Templates

When you don't want to use commercially made templates, you can make your own templates for the Drunkard's Path. There are three parts to the template-making process: drawing or copying the pattern, transferring the pattern to template material, and cutting out the templates. If you are interested in copying some ready-made designs, check the back of this book; you will find several sizes of templates for making the Drunkard's Path. Remember: Photocopies, depending on the copy machine's capabilities, may be slightly distorted from the originals. It is

Figure 5.
Supplies needed to
make your own
templates.

well worth your time to ensure the correct size of all templates before cutting any fabric. Measure and re-measure!

To make your own templates, you will need paper and pencil, a ruler, a compass with pencil, template plastic, a permanent marking pen (fine tip), scissors, and ⅛" hole punch (see Figure 5).

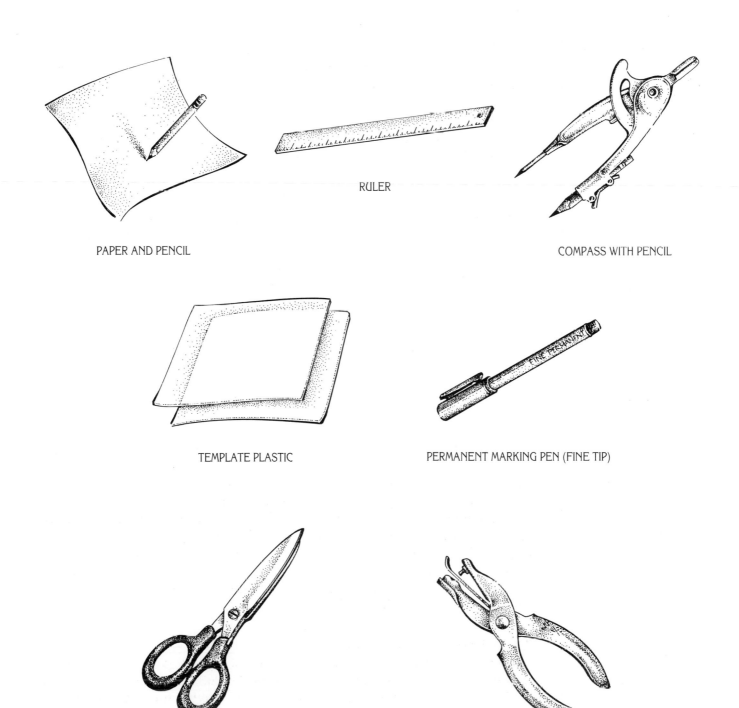

PAPER AND PENCIL RULER COMPASS WITH PENCIL

TEMPLATE PLASTIC PERMANENT MARKING PEN (FINE TIP)

SCISSORS ⅛" HOLE PUNCH

The plastic I prefer for my templates is a .15mm Mylar®. It is a translucent plastic, which means it is slightly gray but clear enough so I can see through to the fabrics underneath. This is especially important when I am placing a template to catch a certain flower or a stripe on the fabric.

To draw Drunkard's Path templates, first consider the size block you want to work with in your quilt. If it is to be one of many blocks, as in a sampler quilt, the Drunkard's Path needs to be the same size as the other blocks. Since the majority of Drunkard's Path variations are based on a four-by-four grid, find the size of one unit of the block by dividing the size of the block by four. (See Figure 6.) For example while a 12" Drunkard's Path is composed of 3" units, a 14" Drunkard's Path would have 3½" units.

Figure 6.
A Drunkard's Path block breaks down into squares.

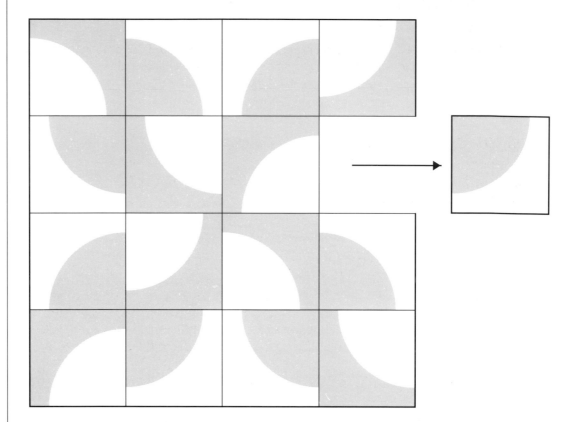

Don't let an odd-size block throw you. For extra help in drafting blocks, refer to my earlier book, *Crosspatch*. If you are impatient and are faced with an awkward-size block, say 17⅜", do the following. First, cut a square of plain paper exactly 17⅜" square. Fold it carefully in half and crease, then fold it in half again. The square will be in quarters and will look like a little book. Fold the "book" in half once, then once more. Crease at each fold. When you unfold the paper, it will be marked in a four-by-four grid. (See Figure 7.) Although this is not as exact as drafting, it is still a tried and true method and will get you the basic unit size of any Drunkard's Path block. Once you are sure of the unit size, use the ruler and draw a square that size on paper.

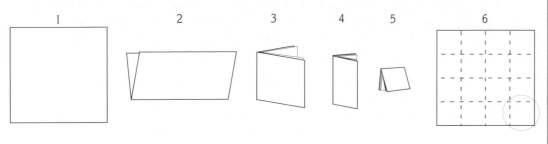

Figure 7.
*Finding the size of
any Drunkard's Path
square unit.*

1. Cut a square of paper the exact size of the desired block (no seam allowances).
2. Fold the square in half (a rectangle).
3. Fold the rectangle in half again. It will look like a little book.
4. Fold the "book" in half.
5. Crease the half-book over.
6. Unfold the square. The four-by-four grid (sixteen little squares) is creased in the paper. One unit of the grid is the size of one unit of the Drunkard's Path block.

Getting the Right Curve in the Drunkard's Path

The next step is dividing the square unit with a true quarter-circle curve. A compass is the best tool for this. Draw a square the size of the Drunkard's Path unit, then follow the steps in Figure 8.

1. Position the point of the compass at the lower left corner of the square and open the compass about three-quarters up the vertical side. The measurement of the size of the quarter-circle curve does not need to be exact. Since this is the prototype for all the curves of the Drunkard's Path block, the other curves will match this first line.

2. Set the pencil point at the vertical side, then swing the compass down to the bottom line of the square in a smooth arc.

3. A true quarter-circle curve.

Figure 8.
*Dividing the square
unit of the Drunkard's
Path with a true
quarter-circle.*

13

Figure 9.
When curves that are not true quarter-circles are used, one of the following may happen:

A lumpy-looking Solomon's Puzzle block indicates more than a quarter-circle curve in the template. Where the curves intersect, there are lobed shapes at the corners of the block.

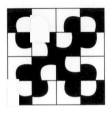

A Solomon's Puzzle block that looks "stretched." When over-large curves are used (less than a true quarter-circle), the curves cannot meet to make true circle shapes.

It is paramount that the curve in a Drunkard's Path block be a true quarter-circle. Many of the block variations, such as Solomon's Puzzle or Baby Bunting, require that curves meet within the block to form other shapes—half-circles, three-quarter circles, whole circles. If the templates used do *not* have a true quarter-circle curve, the results can be odd-looking blocks with lobe-shaped curves (more than a quarter-circle curve) or blocks that have "stretched" curves (less than a quarter-circle curve) and that seem to be stepping out of the block. See Figure 9.

In most antique Drunkard's Path quilts, the stretched block is more common then the lumpy curve. Instead of a compass (which might not have been a readily available tool), the quiltmaker of the past reached for a handy household item to trace the curve on her Drunkard's Path template. If she followed the directions in the Ladies Art Company booklet, for example, she used a saucer or dinner plate. Depending on where she positioned the plate over the drawing of the square, the curve was often over-large, i.e., not a true quarter-circle. If she later pieced a classic Drunkard's Path block, none of the curves would meet and the less-than-perfect templates presented no problem. Only with a block such as Solomon's Puzzle would the inaccurate drafting have been evident.

If you are enamored of the stretched look of the antique Drunkard's Path quilts, then using templates with over-large curves will enhance the effect that the blocks are stepping out of the quilt. (See Photo 5.) If you don't like that stretched look, then measure carefully for a true quarter-circle.

Marking Pinning Points

Once the quarter-circle curve has been drawn on the square, the next step is to mark the dots that indicate the pinning points. With the pinning points marked on both templates, you will be able to pin the pieces together without bunching. Pinning evenly will make for smooth sewing, whether by hand or machine.

From now on, the quarter-circle template piece will be referred to as the *A* template. The wing-shaped remainder is the *B* template. Refer to Figure 10 for directions for marking the pinning dots and tracing the templates on plastic.

FABRIC

And now on to the calculation, buying, and preparation of fabrics for your Drunkard's Path quilt. Let me remind you that *nothing* connected with this subject is a rule. Every quilter has her own opinions—these are mine.

Calculating Fabrics

The easiest method for figuring how much fabric to buy for your Drunkard's Path quilt is to work backwards from the desired size of the finished piece. If you want to make a classic Drunkard's Path in two colors, the process is fairly simple. It goes like this:

A) Suppose you want to make a Drunkard's Path quilt to use on a double bed. The finished size will be 90" x 108", that is, two-and-a-half yards wide by three yards long. You should:

B) Multiply 2½ by 3 yards. The result is 7½ yards—7½ *square* yards to be exact.

C) Add a half-yard for seam allowance and shrinkage, to make an even eight yards.

Figure 10. Completing the templates for Drunkard's Path

PARTS OF THE DRUNKARD'S PATH UNIT

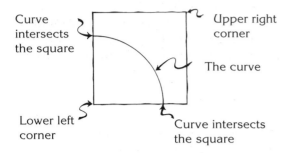

Curve intersects the square

Upper right corner

The curve

Lower left corner

Curve intersects the square

GETTING THE CENTER DOT RIGHT

 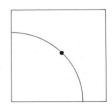

Lay the edge of a ruler from the lower left to upper right corner. Where the ruler crosses the curve, mark a dot.

The dot is the center pinning point.

MORE DOTS

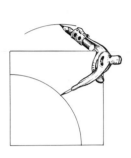 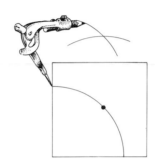 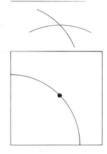 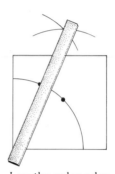 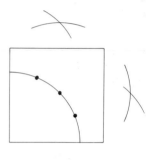

Keep compass at same setting and put the point at the center dot. Mark an arc above the square.

Set the compass point at the intersection of the curve and square. Draw an arc.

The arcs cross.

Lay the ruler edge from the lower left corner to the cross of the arcs. Where the ruler crosses the curve, mark a dot.

Repeat for the other side.

ON TO THE PLASTIC

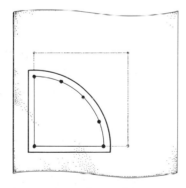 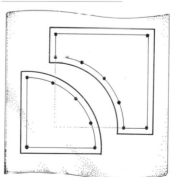 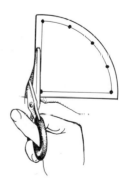 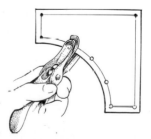

Darken all the dots on the drawing as indicated.

Lay a piece of template plastic over the drawing. Trace the first template (*A*) with dots and add ¼" to all sides.

Move over the plastic and trace the second template (*B*). Add ¼" lines.

Cut out the templates on the ¼" lines.

Punch out the dots.

D) Divide eight by two (the number of fabrics used in the quilt). You will need four yards of each fabric.

Since almost all modern fabrics are 44"/45" wide, you will actually have more than eight yards of fabric. The calculations for any quilt cannot take into account all possible factors. If you are prone to cut a few pieces wrong, prefer directional fabrics, or want borders on the quilt, then additional yardage is required.

Every quiltmaker should take the time to figure, or at least re-check, the yardages given for making a particular quilt. This precaution can avoid the unpleasant affliction known as Lost Fabric Syndrome (LFS). Gambling that you will later be able to find more of one of your fabrics leads to haunting the flat-fold tables at the discount fabric stores and undignified scenes at the counter of the local quilt shop. Lost Fabric Syndrome can be recognized when a distraught woman, without any provocation, frantically pulls a scrap of fabric from her purse and thrusts it at you, demanding, "Have you seen this fabric?!"

Purchasing Fabrics

My personal rule of thumb for purchasing fabrics is rather broad. If the fabric is an unusual (read ugly) color, I purchase a quarter-yard piece. Accent colors that I use regularly merit half-yard cuts. Fabrics I like are bought in one-yard chunks. Those fabrics I love are purchased at three-yard whacks—minimum. A stripe with border possibilities is bought in a three-and-a-half-yard cut. On occasion, I buy in larger quantities. Once, a cornflower blue cotton printed with tiny white birds induced a severe case of fabric lust in me. I remember it well—I was nineteen at the time, not even a quilter yet—because I bought the whole bolt. Sometimes it's just better to give in than to resist. The factor that ostensibly determines how much fabric I buy is the requirements of the project on hand; in reality, my true limitation is the amount of cash I am carrying.

The only advice I can offer others about purchasing fabrics is this: If you are the type of quiltmaker who only feels comfortable knowing ahead of time exactly how much fabric you will need, then the extra work of calculating fabrics prior to starting will preserve your sanity and save you from LFS. Purchase all the fabrics you *imagine* you might need before you cut a single piece of your Drunkard's Path.

Preparation of the Fabrics

There are many opinions on the best method of preparing fabrics for quiltmaking. What works for me is to machine-wash all the fabrics in warm water with a mild soap. I do not use fabric softener. Small scraps I wash in a lingerie bag. Then I semi-dry the fabrics, rescuing them to be ironed smooth (and I don't use any dryer sheets). For the most part, you will be safe if, as you prepare your fabrics, you think ahead to the eventual use—the wear and tear—that your quilt is likely to receive. Prepare your fabrics with the future of your quilt in mind.

A PLAN FOR THE QUILT

No matter what your usual quilting work style—whether it's casual design-as-you-go or a carefully thought-out process—a Drunkard's Path quilt is one project where you really *must* take a little time to make a diagram of the basic block, and then a rough sketch of the whole quilt. If you like, use colored pencils or pens to color the drawing. Jot notations about the arrangement of the blocks or observations about the fabrics to one side. Paste down postage-stamp-size swatches of the fabrics. Think of this drawing not as a hard and fast plan for your quilt, with no room for variation or change. Rather, imagine that the drawing represents general guidelines for the project. The drawing will be a special help as you begin piecing your Drunkard's Path. You may get to feeling so sure of your skills that you neglect to refer to the drawing as you work. At that point, the Drunkard's Path block will reassert its baffling nature, and you will find you have incorrectly assembled a block. Perhaps that is how the tidy English Mill Wheel became a Drunkard's Path in the first place! To avoid wayward Drunkard's Path blocks, check the blocks against the drawing at the end of a day's work.

CONTINUING WORK

When you have made the first Drunkard's Path block, examine it closely. Are you satisfied with the result? Pin the block on a wall and step back and look at it. Consider the relation of the fabrics to one another. Would you be pleased with a whole quilt in those colors? A wonderful trick to visualize that single block as a whole quilt is an ingenious little device called a Multi-View Lens. As you look through the lens, the image of the block will be multiplied many times. You almost see your quilt before you have made it.

If you like that first Drunkard's Path block, then cut out enough pieces for four or five more blocks. Usually, I spend an hour cutting and then several hours sewing. A full day of either of these activities is boring and tiring, so trade off these tasks. Unless you are quite sure you will follow the drawing, do not assemble the blocks in rows for a while. Who knows what good ideas you might get as you are making blocks? With the Drunkard's Path pattern, there are always interesting choices waiting around the next curve!

*My older sister,
Mary Frances Peddie,
the reluctant cowgirl.
Cairo, Egypt, c. 1947.*

There are two approaches to designing with the Drunkard's Path pattern. The first method is to play around with the elements of the block itself, in other words, from the inside out. The second approach is to rearrange the set of the quilt, that is, the number of blocks and their placement. Designing with the set is designing from the outside in.

Most quiltmakers are familiar with the set designing approach. Experimenting with the arrangements of the blocks, after they have been pieced, is natural in the quilt assembly process. With the Drunkard's Path, many sets are possible.

The traditional set for the Drunkard's Path is to sew the blocks side-by-side. Then the curves of the individual blocks seem to connect and the quilt has allover waves. Sometimes borders are added to frame the patchwork and to increase the size of the quilt (Figure 11 and Photo 1).

Figure 11.
The traditional set for Drunkard's Path blocks. The curves merge to become allover waves across the quilt.

When Drunkard's Path blocks set side-by-side seem too busy for the taste of the quiltmaker, then alternate plain blocks offer some visual relief. Alternate blocks with only quarter-circles at the corners can also be used to link the pieced blocks (Figure 12A and B, and Photos 5 and 7).

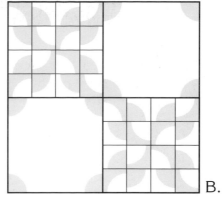

A.

B.

Figure 12A.
Pieced blocks set with alternate plain blocks allow for fancy quilting designs.

Figure 12B.
Pieced blocks set with alternate blocks with quarter-circles at their corners.

Since the main attraction of the Drunkard's Path pattern for most quiltmakers is the meandering "paths," the blocks are seldom set apart with sashing strips. Some Drunkard's Path variations that seem contained within the block (rather than stretched across the block in an X shape) such as Solomon's Puzzle were more often seen set with sashing. Two sets are pictured in this book. One is the classic strip-and-little-square sashing seen in Mary Jo Houston Braun's baby quilt (Figure 13 and Photo 9), and the other is shown in Figure 14. The second sort of sashing, called "Garden Maze," is not a common quilt set today.

Figure 13.
A Solomon's Puzzle-type block, here called Tumbleweed, set with sashing and squares in Mary Jo Houston Braun's baby quilt. See Photo 9.

19

Figure 14.
This block, called
Fool's Puzzle by its
maker, is set with a
"Garden Maze" type
of sashing.

Drunkard's Path is often found in a sampler quilt, since it is the ideal block for the new quilter to practice sewing a curved seam. An idea for getting lots of practice with curves is what I call the *One-Block Sampler* (Figure 15). This is a sampler quilt in which the same pattern is rearranged in different ways. See Photo 15.

Figure 15.
The One-Block Sampler
has five variations of the
same block —
Rob Peter to Pay Paul,
Illinois Rose, the classic
Drunkard's Path,
King Tut's Crown, and
The Dove. The diagonal
set has its ancestor in
Center Diamond quilts
of the Pennsylvania
Amish. See also
Photo 15.

Set styles can be inspired by quilts from other cultures and ethnic traditions. When patchwork blocks (in this case, Rob Peter to Pay Paul blocks) are set in vertical or horizontal rows separated by sashing, the effect might be reminiscent of either the strippy quilts of Great Britain or some examples of African-American quilts (Figure 16 and Photo 13).

Figure 16.
Rob Peter to Pay Paul blocks in vertical rows separated by strips. Strippy quilts from England and African-American quilts inspired this arrangement. See also Photo 13.

The Center Diamond quilts of the Pennsylvania Amish present an interesting format for Drunkard's Path blocks. The Center Diamond is a natural medallion and effortlessly concentrates the viewer's attention on the quilt. The *One-Block Sampler* has obviously borrowed from the Center Diamond, as has the tiny Drunkard's Path block set on point in the miniature quilt (Photos 14 and 15).

When designing on the diagonal (as the examples illustrate), some half-blocks are required to fill out the quilt to a square. Rather than cutting Drunkard's Path blocks in half, use plain triangles of the same size. Hacking off the patchwork looks awkward and it is a shame to waste your work.

Drunkard's Path blocks can be extended by the addition of partial blocks. *Whirling Mandala* is four Drunkard's Path blocks with half-blocks at the north-south-east west points of the patchwork. The visual movement of the blocks seems to leap over the first border and only the second border, much wider and a dark color, can contain the quilt (Figure 17 and Photo16)

Figure 17.
*Whirling Mandala.
Four Drunkard's Path
blocks plus partial
blocks over the first
border. See Photo 16.*

Another set, seldom seen, is the "half-block drop." Drunkard's Path blocks (in this case, the Sunshine and Shadows variation) are sewn in a vertical column. A second vertical row is set half a block lower than the first strip of blocks. The eye of the viewer moves up and down over the surface of the quilt following the zigzag design (Figure 18). This idea of not setting the blocks even with one another is carried even further in an allover pattern using the "three-quarter-block drop." The blocks are then joined by large rectangles that equal half the size of a patchwork block. This variation is called Drunkard's Patchwork (Figure 19).

*Figure 18.
The half-block drop set.*

*A single Sunshine and
Shadows block.*

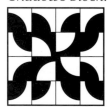

Figure 19.
More Sunshine and
Shadows blocks in a
three-quarter-block drop
set with large plain
rectangles. This was
sometimes called
Drunkard's Patchwork.

Other patchwork patterns may be paired with Drunkard's Path blocks. The little crosspatch quilt *Meteor Shower* combines Drunkard's Path units with stars, resulting in the effect of falling stars with "tails" (Figure 20 and Photo 17).

Figure 20.
Meteor Shower is a
crosspatch of stars plus
Drunkard's Path units.
The curves seem to be
"tails" of the falling
stars.

Working with the units in the block—from the inside out—also yields interesting results. Figure 21 shows three border possibilities. The first two borders are derived exclusively from quarter-circle-in-a-square units. The third border needs additional plain squares to complete the design.

Figure 21.
Borders. For more
inspiration on using the
Drunkard's Path in
borders, see Gregor
Gamble's Devil's Puzzle
and Mary Jo Dalrymple's
Migration (Photos 22
and 36). Borders A and
B use only the quarter-
circle-in-a-square units
of the traditional
Drunkard's Path.

Border B was used in
Eclipse (Photo 20).

This larger border (C)
needs small, plain
squares, as well as the
quarter circle-in-a-square
units, to make this
formal baroque-looking
border.

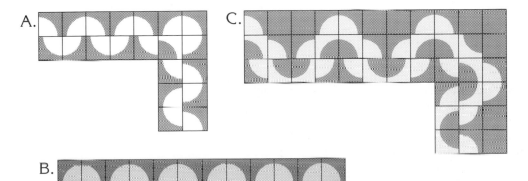

A.

C.

B.

Although the majority of Drunkard's Path blocks are based on a four-by-four grid, new blocks can be designed when other grids are used. The quilt *Gyre* by Bonnie Bus began as a Drunkard's Path, plus plain squares, drawn over a seven-by-seven grid (Figure 22 and Photo 18). In the *Happy Sampler* (Photo 24), Marsha McCloskey designed the block Around the Mountain on a three-by-three grid. Other new quarter-circle-in-a-square blocks are Puzzle Boxes by Jan Halgrimson, Mirage by Cynthia Buettner, and an amusing Turtle in a Puddle block. The Turtle is a *Kansas City Star* pattern, while I added the triangles to make the "in a Puddle" frame. Likewise inspired by the Drunkard's Path, I designed Opening Valentines, Toll House and Plank Road (quartered by a cross), and Scallop Shells (Figure 23 and Photo 24).

Cynthia Buettner, the designer of the Mirage block, has written an excellent booklet entitled *Patchwork Parade*. Many of her patterns have a

Figure 22.
Gyre is based on a seven-by-seven grid. See Photo 18.

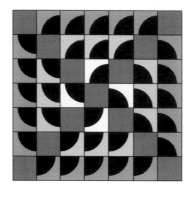

Figure 23.
See The Happy Sampler (Photo 24).

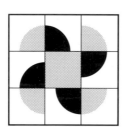

Around the Mountain by Marsha McCloskey

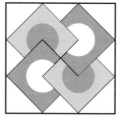

Puzzle Boxes by Jan Halgrimson

Mirage by Cynthia Buettner

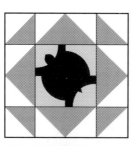

Turtle in a Puddle from the Kansas City Star (with help from Pepper Cory)

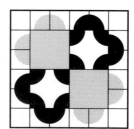

Opening Valentines by Pepper Cory

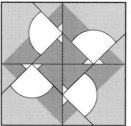

Scallop Shells by Pepper Cory

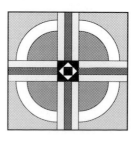

Toll House and Plank Road by Pepper Cory

quarter-circle-in-a-square theme. (See "Resources" at the end of this book for ordering information.)

The Drunkard's Path has rarely been used in an album or friendship quilt. However, some Amish quilters were not daunted by the block (or its name) and they boldly added their signatures to the blocks in embroidery floss (Photo 25). A modern quiltmaker, Ida Copeland, likewise experimented with a Drunkard's Path variation in a scrap-style friendship quilt (Figure 24 and Photo 26). While Ida supplied the solid red to unify the blocks, her friends from the Harbor Springs, Michigan, Wednesday Group pieced the blocks for her. This pattern has both a small and a large quarter-circle in two units. The remaining units have only the large quarter-circle. The effect is a wonderful wobbling "walk" all over the quilt. *Flying Under Radar* is a charm quilt top I made as the result of a twice-a-month quilt group. Although not a charm quilt in the strictest sense (the pattern employs more than one template shape), *Flying Under Radar* contains 949 fabrics, all different (Figure 25 and Photo 27).

One intriguing Drunkard's Path relation is the maze pattern Snake's Trail (sometimes called Drunkard's Trail). The blocks, with their double circles in opposing corners, could be arranged in many maze sets (Figure 26). This quilt was almost exclusively made in the southern United States and the directions for setting the blocks in the maze were carefully hoarded and passed from quiltmaker to quiltmaker. One maze set is graphed out in Figure 26 (see also Photo 29). Another variation of the Drunkard's Path with two quarter-circles in a unit is Bow and Arrows (Figure 27 and Photo 30). Pieced in an informal scrap style, the color counter-change blocks make for a twinkling graphic design.

Figure 24.
Ida Copeland's
Friendship block.

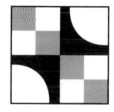

Figure 25.
The block for
Flying Under Radar
is a Drunkard's Path
variation called
Pictures in the Stair-
well from the Kansas
City Star.

Figure 26.
Depending on the
source, this block
was recognized as a
Drunkard's Path
variation called
Drunkard's Trail.
The maze set for
Snake's Trail blocks
is sometimes called
Snake in the Hollow
(see Photo 29).

Figure 27.
Bow and Arrows
has also been called
Steeplechase
(Photo 30).

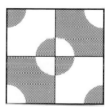

Snake's Trail
block.

DEVELOPING A DESIGNING ATTITUDE

Of all the steps in the quiltmaking process, the experience of designing has been explored the least. Don't get me wrong—basic how-to and the manipulation of tools is indeed useful knowledge. However, designing—considering ways to make quilts that express your unique viewpoint—is much less real and accessible to the average quilter. Books can instruct, illustrations can diagram, but designing requires three vital, yet intangible, ingredients.

The first requisite in becoming a better designer is open-mindedness. The enemies of open-mindedness are legion. Some traditionalists believe they are obliged to defend antique quilts: "But the pattern is *always* done in blue and white!" Other quilters are critical about new concepts such as the architectural style of many contemporary quilts: "All quilts should be pretty, soft, and feminine!" Still others nitpick methods. Does this complaint sound familiar? "It's not a *real* quilt unless every stitch has been sewn by hand!"

Coming from a traditional quiltmaking background myself, I empathize with this reluctance to experiment. Let's admit it—we are all a bit afraid of change. Perhaps we fear that accepting new concepts means we must abandon all our old ideas about quiltmaking. What if the new stuff doesn't work? But adopting an open mind is not difficult. All it means is that when faced with something new or radically different in quiltmaking, we do not automatically dismiss the new idea. Consciously staying open-minded is the first step toward becoming a better quilt designer.

The next element in the designing process is desire. Desire is equal parts competitiveness, energy to experiment, and the hope of leaving a personal legacy of work. Desire is a very strong unfathomable force that every quiltmaker must bring to the process of designing.

The last ingredient of designing is The Plan. The Plan can be very simple—such as acting on some of the suggestions in this chapter for rethinking the sets of Drunkard's Path quilts or manipulating the elements within the Drunkard's Path block.

But here is the truth about designing—no Fairy Quiltmother will bop you on the head and immediately solve your quilt designing dilemmas. It is up to you. The process of designing is too subtle and complex to adequately explain in words. But perhaps you can recognize that silent "Click!" of comprehension that happens just before the happy quiltmaker rushes off to try her bright idea in cloth. That joyful feeling is universal to all creative people, and you are bound to experience that gratifying "Click!" more and more as your designing skills develop.

One final word about designing. You might well ask, "If I'm going to be so open-minded, excited about the process of designing, and all set to sew, why would I need a Plan at all?" You need a Plan because when you want to kick up your heels and break the rules, you've got to know what the rules are. When it comes to your Drunkard's Path quilt, The Plan is your invitation to tinker. The Plan gives you permission to dream of new quilts and entices you to change your work even when you are in the midst of it. The Plan is the best antidote to boredom and frustration that I know.

SEWING THE CURVE

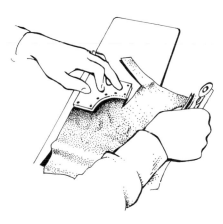

Although I hope you have read this far because you just can't put this book down, when you are ready to actually start sewing a Drunkard's Path block, these are the pages to keep in front of you as you work. If you have skipped to this chapter, do take the time to go back and read "Before You Sew." These directions assume that you have prepared your fabrics, your sewing machine is in good working order, and that you have made (or bought) templates.

If you plan to use commercially made templates and a rotary cutter to cut your pieces, use a cutting mat that's an easy size to move, and use the small-blade cutter. The big-wheel cutter will not cut around the concave curve of the template. Don't even try with the big blade—you'll just hack up your fabric.

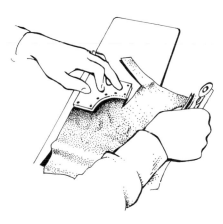

1) Fold the fabric double, matching selvages. Cut the corner first. The perpendicular cuts can overlap. Don't get your hand in an awkward position to cut. Instead, move the cutting mat to make the job easier. Applying little sticky sandpaper dots to the underside of the templates will keep them from moving on the fabrics.

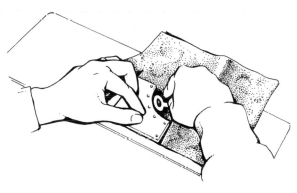

3) Cutting the inside (concave) curve. Do not apply so much pressure that your template wiggles. A firm, but not frantic, grip on the cutter plus a steady downward pressure will easily cut the double layer. Need I say the blade of your cutter should be nice and sharp?

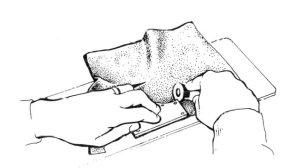

2) The last straight line cut.

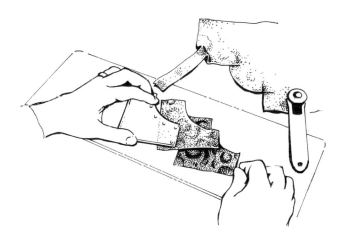

4) Two pieces cut at a time.

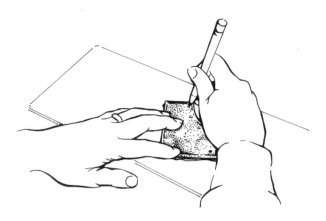

5) Mark the pinning dots by marking through the template's holes. Use a washable pencil and always mark on the *wrong* side of the pieces.

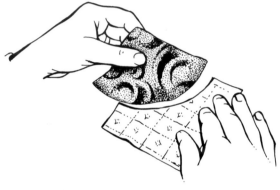

6) When the pieces are laid next to each other, they don't seem to fit. Do not panic. The seam allowances produce this illusion.

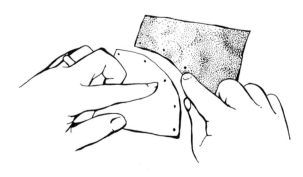

7) Turn the pieces over. The dots marked on the back sides will assure matched pinning points.

8) Homemade templates may also be used. These have lines drawn with a nonsmudge pen and holes punched with a ⅛" punch. Refer to "Before You Sew" for directions for making these templates.

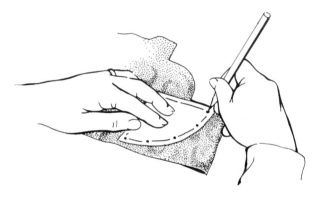

9) On the back of the fabrics, trace around the templates and dot through the holes.

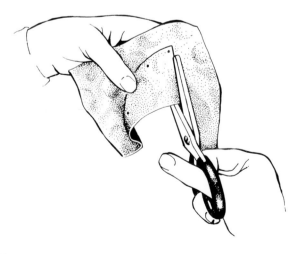

10) Using scissors, cut out the pieces along the marked lines. Do not estimate any extra fabric for seam allowance. These templates have the seam allowance included.

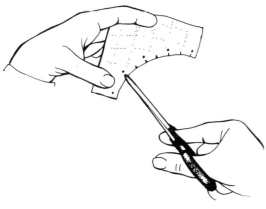

11) On both rotary-cut and scissors-cut *B* (concave) pieces, clip just behind the dots and once between the dots. Do *not* take a full ¼" clip. Rather make it a smidge over ⅛".

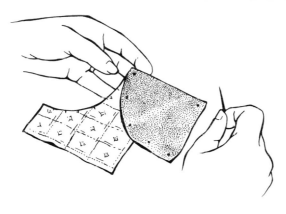

12) Starting the pinning. Flip over the *A* piece and line it up on *B* as indicated.

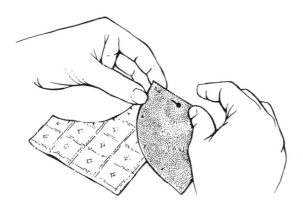

13) Pin at the dot. I like long silk pins; I pin holding the head of the pin toward my right hand and the point toward the seam.

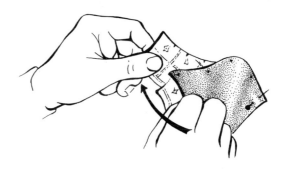

14) This step is important. Take the *A* piece and swing its unpinned corner to meet its mate on *B*. Pin.

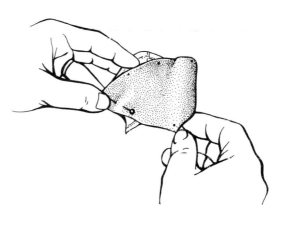

15) The pieces will be bunched up in your hand.

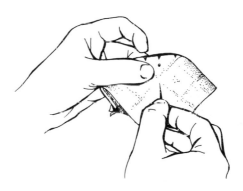

16) Turn over the pieces so that *B* faces you. Align the pieces by taking a pin and spearing both pieces through their center dots. Hold the pieces in position, take the pin out, and re-pin with the point toward the seam.

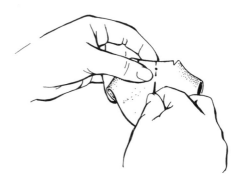

17) The pin at the center dot in place.

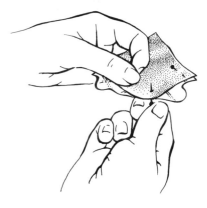

18) At all the dots on the curve, spear through the pieces and re-pin. Sometimes you'll want to turn over the pieces and check that the dots on both pieces line up.

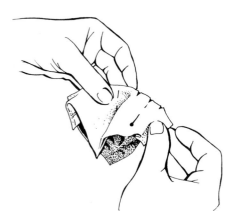

19) More pins in. Notice the fullness immediately starts to be brought under control as pins are added.

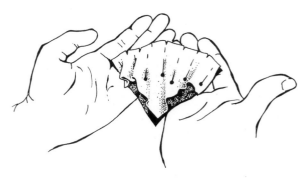

20) Use as many pins as needed. As you become more skilled, you will use fewer pins.

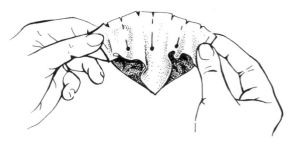

21) The two pieces are now pinned together. The clips have allowed the curve of *B* to stretch and the pinning has solved the fitting dilemma.

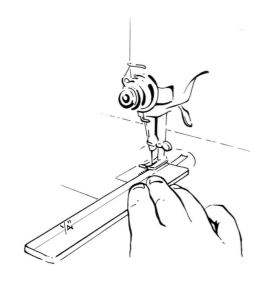

22) When sewing by machine, be sure your seam is an exact quarter-inch. Check by measuring with a ruler ¼" from where the needle comes down. You can make your own guide by putting down a 2" length of masking tape on the plate of the sewing machine. When feeding pieces through the machine, take care that the fabric just touches the edge of the tape.

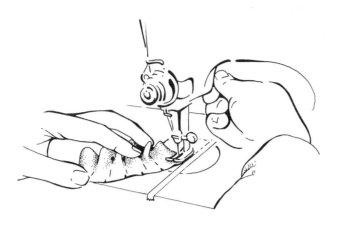

23) Sew with the *B* piece facing you. The tiny points of the silk pins may protrude slightly over the sewing line. The needle will usually avoid the points since they are very small. Start stitching at the outer dot.

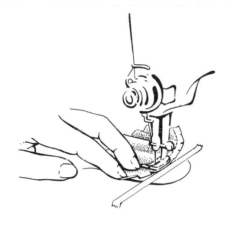

24) Continue around the curve intersecting the marked dots on the fabric.

26) Pins out...ready to unfold.

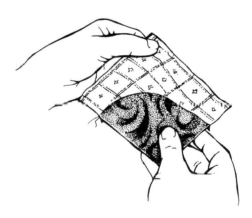

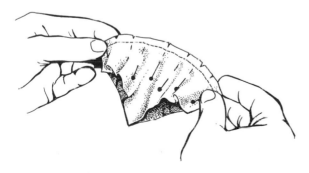

25) The seam is sewn and the pins are still in.

27) A square with a quarter-circle— the perfect curved seam. Ready to try another one?

After all the preparation, cutting, and pinning, the act of stitching seems almost anticlimactic. Sewing will be a breeze if you follow the preceding steps carefully.

Hand piecing needs preparation as well. Follow the cutting and pinning steps above to #21, then continue with these steps. Start by threading your needle with a color thread that matches the darkest fabric or a color that blends with both fabrics. Do not use quilting thread for hand piecing. A lighter weight (about #50) cotton or poly/cotton blend thread that does not tend to knot is best. Incidentally, I prefer a #11 Sharp needle. It is as thin as a quilting needle, but longer so that more stitches can be taken at a time.

28) Holding the pinned pieces so that the curve curves away from you, take a couple of stitches toward the dot at the left of the curve. At the dot, push the needle out.

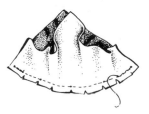

30) When you come to the end dot, reverse the pieces and backstitch a couple of stitches.

29) Turn the pieces so that the curve faces toward you. Taking an even running stitch, sew around the curve without stopping.

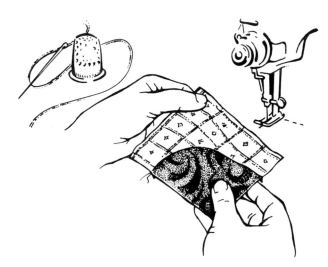

31) Take out the pins and voila! The curve is sewn beautifully by hand as well as machine.

After sewing the curve has been mastered (and practice is the best method to assure success), all that is left is to assemble the unit squares in the Drunkard's Path variation of your choice. Refer to a diagram of the block as you sew the squares together. I cannot stress this caution enough. There are many antique Drunkard's Path quilts that display mismatched piecing. Unless you don't mind answering rude suggestions as to your state of sobriety, sew the units of your Drunkard's Path blocks together carefully.

1. *Old Maid's Puzzle*
The Drunkard's Path was usually called by this name when Amish quiltmakers used the pattern. This beautiful Amish quilt, from northern Indiana and dated 1939, is quilted in white thread. From the collection of Rebecca Haarer.

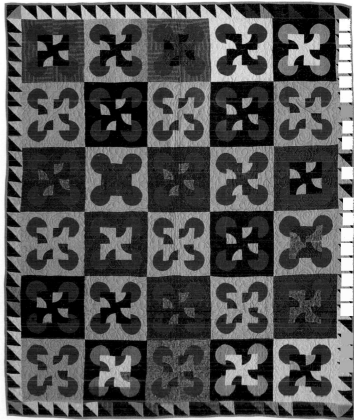

2. *Solomon's Puzzle*
Pieced entirely of wools, this graphic quilt, complemented by a sawtooth border, was quilted by machine. Found in Missouri but supposedly from Iowa, it was made in the 1930s or '40s. Collection of the author.

3. *Drunkard's Path* **(alternate block)**
A Pennsylvania quiltmaker in the 1930s
made this scrappy blue-and-white
charmer. Collection of the author.

4. *Rob Peter to Pay Paul*
This is the oldest quilt in my collection. Made between 1840 and 1860,
it was bought in Pennsylvania — just
in time before it was cut into teddy
bears! Collection of the author.

5. *Stepping Out*

A quilt with two Drunkard's Path blocks using templates with a "stretched" look (the curve is larger than a true quarter-circle). Set with simple squares of dark fabrics. The stretched look is accentuated by the Drunkard's Path units that meet at the corners of the blocks and the additional units that cross into the border at the upper left and lower right. Designing and piecing by Pepper Cory; quilting by Judy Schimmel.

6. *Drunkard's Path*

The quilt pictured on the cover of *Happy Trails*. In mint condition, this quilt, from York, Pennsylvania, was made around 1890. The quiltmaker added bright pink and green borders but ran out of both fabrics on the last border. Collection of the author.

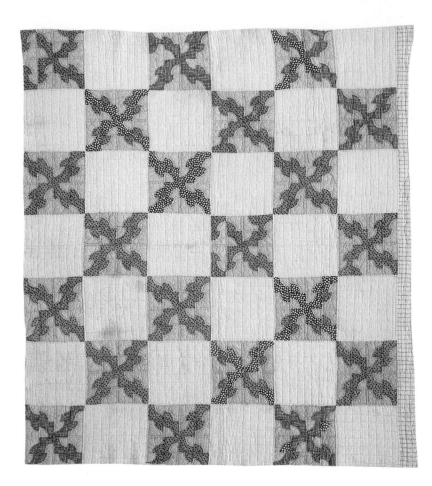

7. *Drunkard's Path*
This well-worn quilt, made in Iowa in the 1930s, shows the quiltmaker's efforts to simplify the mystery of the Drunkard's Path pattern. Set with alternate plain blocks of white, the quilt is certainly less busy than many Drunkard's Path quilts, but the baffling nature of the block has still reasserted itself — several of the blocks are incorrectly pieced! Collection of the author.

8. *Love Ring*
A baby quilt, made from recycled blocks bought at an Amish auction. Piecing by Pepper Cory; quilting by Doris Lucas.

9. *Tumbleweed*
Made by Mary Jo Houston Braun in 1990, this baby quilt has two-color blocks separated by sashing, then brought together by the en-circling cable quilting on the outer border. Collection of Nancy and Marvin Suit. Photo by Mark Eifert.

10. *Around the World*
Although this pattern is better known as Drunkard's Path, the Amish quiltmaker named this pattern. The color change in the blocks illustrates the Amish frugality with fabrics: "A blue is a blue is a blue." Made in 1989 in northern Indiana. Collection of the author.

11. *Wonder of the World* (also *Around the World*)
A small quilt experimenting with large, loud plaids. Designing and piecing by Pepper Cory; quilting by Ada Brower.

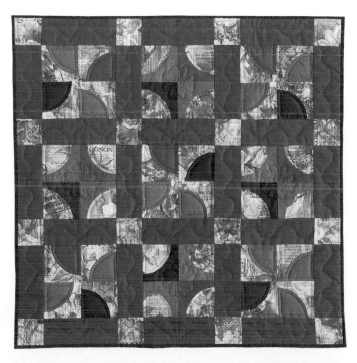

12. *Wonder of the World* (also *Around the World*)
The blocks are broken up by sashing which changes the look of the pattern entirely. Compare this quilt with the previous two quilts. Designing and piecing by Pepper Cory; quilting by Norine Antuck.

13. *Rob Peter to Pay Paul*
Antique Rob Peter to Pay Paul blocks (made in the 1930s) were found at a flea market. The blocks were set in three vertical columns separated by a striped fabric, then bordered a couple of times. This set is similar to the strippy quilts found in Great Britain and also some African-American quilts. Setting by Pepper Cory; quilting by Shirley A. Thompson.

14. *Miniature Drunkard's Path*
One miniature block, set on point, makes for a tiny quilt. Designing and piecing by Pepper Cory; quilting by Nancy Myers.

15. *The One-Block Sampler*
Five 16" Drunkard's Path variations combine in this quilt—Rob Peter to Pay Paul, Illinois Rose, classic Drunkard's Path, King Tut's Crown, and The Dove. Designing and piecing by Pepper Cory; quilting by Louise Mueller. Collection of the author.

16. *Whirling Mandala*
Four scrappy Drunkard's Path blocks are extended by the addition of partial blocks at the north-south-east-west points of the quilt. The partial blocks seem to cross over the first border but are contained by the second, darker border. Designing and piecing by Pepper Cory; quilting by Kathy Curtis.

17. *Meteor Shower*
A little quilt combining Drunkard's Path units with an eight-point star block. Designing and piecing by Pepper Cory; quilting by Ruth Dukelow; binding by Nancy Myers. Collection of the author.

18. *Gyre*
A Drunkard's Path variation based on a seven-by-seven grid. Designing by Pepper Cory; piecing and further designing by Bonnie Bus; quilting by Marti Caterino.

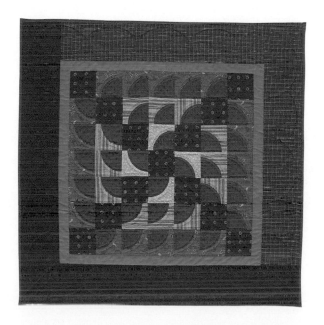

19. *Drunkard's Path*

A great example of a scrap style combined with expert quilting. This gem is from Indiana and was probably made in the 1890s. Contrast this piece to the Amish quilt in Photo 1, and see how the eclectic use of different fabrics has softened the jagged lines of the Drunkard's Path pattern. Compare this with *Eclipse* (facing page), which uses many of the same colors but is a modern scrap quilt, both in the international diversity of its fabrics and in its block arrangement. Collection of Ardis and Robert James. Photo courtesy of Ardis and Robert James.

20. *Eclipse*
A new scrap quilt, pieced predominantly in the traditional Mill Wheel block. However, the lights and darks are centered at the quilt's middle suggesting the effect of a solar eclipse. A large sun face is quilted at the middle, but it is only visible from the back (dark side) of the quilt. Designing and piecing by Pepper Cory; quilting by Judy Schimmel.

21. *Devil's Puzzle*
A Drunkard's Path variation, this is based on a six-by-six format rather than the usual four-by-four grid. Piecing done in a scrap style by Pepper Cory.

22. *Devil's Puzzle*
This delicate quilt, pieced in blues, green, lavender, and pink, was made by Gregor Gamble. Her quilting highlights the pattern's curves, and the quarter-circles join around the quilt to form bouncing balls bordering the patchwork. From the collection of Helen Gamble.

23. *Kathy Sue's Puzzle*
Louise Mueller made this queen-size quilt as a gift for her daughter-in-law, Kathy Sue. Louise modified the traditional Devil's Puzzle block until the new version had enough white space to satisfy her quilting needs. Collection of Kathy Sue Mueller. Photo by Mark Eifert.

24. *The Happy Sampler*

A small sampler quilt that includes blocks of my own design inspired by the Drunkard's Path plus blocks by other quiltmakers. All of these variations are modern (designed after 1940). The blocks (from upper left down) are Toll House and Plank Road (Pepper Cory), Scallop Shells (Pepper Cory), Mirage (Cynthia Buettner), Opening Valentines (Pepper Cory), Puzzle Boxes (Jan Halgrimson), Turtle in a Puddle (combination of a *Kansas City Star* pattern plus triangles from traditional Toad in a Puddle block), and Around the Mountain (Marsha McCloskey). Piecing by Pepper Cory; quilting by Gail Hill. Collection of the author.

25. *Old Maid's Puzzle*

An Amish friendship quilt from northern Indiana, this was probably made in the 1920s or '30s. The makers of the blocks signed their names in pearl cotton across the blocks. From the collection of Rebecca Haarer.

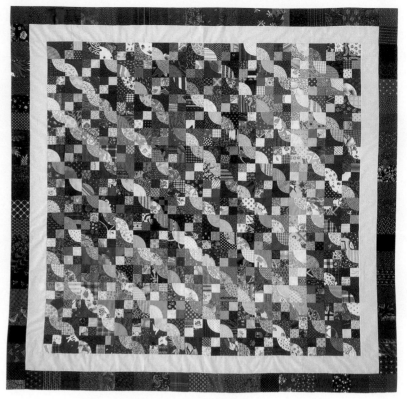

26. *Ida's Friendship Quilt Top*
Inspired by a photo of an antique scrap quilt, Ida Copeland distributed the patterns for this quilt, plus pieces of solid red fabric, to her friends from the Wednesday Quilt Group of Harbor Springs, Michigan. Rare in a group quilt, the artistic composition of the quilt top remains harmonious in spite of many different fabrics. Collection of Ida Copeland.

27. *Flying Under Radar*
A charm quilt top pieced as the result of the Daughters of Charm Quilt Group which met twice monthly the winter of 1990-1991. The pattern cannot be strictly labelled a charm quilt since it employs more than one template, though there *are* 949 different fabrics in the quilt top. The block is Pictures in the Stairwell. After having pieced the top, it seemed to me that the wing-shape appears and disappears throughout the design, reminding me of the Stealth aircraft I had been seeing on television. Designing and piecing by Pepper Cory. Collection of the author.

28. *Rob Peter to Pay Paul* (variation)
Made between 1900 and 1920, this Ohio quilt separates the blocks by bold brown sashing. Collection of the author.

29. *Snake's Trail* (or *Drunkard's Trail*) **set in a Snake in the Hollow Maze**
Almost exclusively made in the rural South, this scrap pattern of the 1930s was a "puzzle" quilt, i.e., special directions were needed to set the blocks together in a maze. The directions were much sought after and carefully passed from one quiltmaker to the next. From Indiana. Collection of the author.

30. *Bow and Arrows*
A scrap pattern that used two quarter-circles in opposing corners in each unit of the block. From Tennessee, it was made around 1900. Collection of the author.

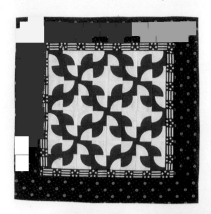

31. *Faux Drunkard's Path*
Using Barbara Brackman's polka-dot shortcut method, this miniature quilt top is an eye-fooler. Refer to the chapter "No-Curve Drunkard's Path" for instructions. Piecing by Pepper Cory.

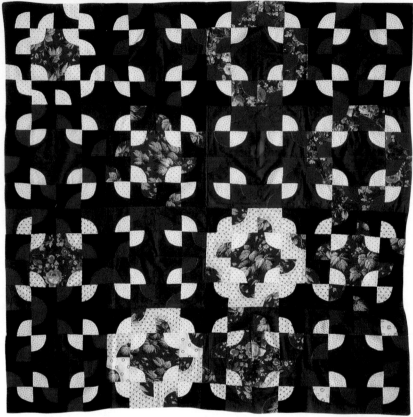

32. *Drunkard's Path* (quilt top)
Dating from about 1910, this Illinois quilt top used cretonne florals, men's shirting fabrics, and several shades of solid red and green. All the curves are top-stitched in white thread. The construction of the top leads me to believe that a seamstress, familiar with the attachments of her sewing machine, used her edge stitcher foot (rather than sew curves) to lap over the pieces to get the quarter-circle shapes. Refer to the chapter "No-Curve Drunkard's Path" for instructions. Collection of the author.

33. *Log Cabin Drunkard's Path*
A small quilt made with Log Cabin blocks that seem to curve. See the chapter "No-Curve Drunkard's Path" for directions. Piecing by Pepper Cory; quilting by Carol Schon. Collection of the author.

34. *Serendipity*

Quilt top designed and pieced by Bonnie Bus. The Drunkard's Path blocks are used as backdrop to the appliqués of ferns and violets. Bonnie named her piece *Serendipity* because she says the design "just happened by accident." Collection of Bonnie Bus.

35. *Drunkard's Path Sampler*

This lovely quilt top combines variations of the Drunkard's Path with a center medallion wreath of grapes and vines (the result of a workshop with Elly Sienkiewicz), embellished with beads and ribbons. Many of the fabrics in the quilt are hand-dyed. Designing and piecing by Cynthia Griewahn of Riverton, Wyoming. Collection of the quiltmaker.

The blocks, reading left to right across the quilt, are:
1) Doves 2) center of Chain Links block 3) Gulls
4) Throwing Star 5) Mushroom Merry-Go-Round
6) Vine of Friendship 7) Drunkard's Path
8) Falling Timbers 9) Rob Peter to Pay Paul
10) more Doves 11) Fool's Puzzle 12) Illinois Rose
13) Baby Bunting variation 14) Whirling Arches
15) center of Devil's Puzzle 16) Falling Waters

36. *Migration*

Made in 1984 by Mary Jo Dalrymple. Inspired by her friend Lila Rostenberg's Drunkard's Path quilt, Mary Jo set out to make a quilt exactly like the one she so admired. However, with the fabrics she chose, the quilt "took wing" by itself and became the birds, sea, and sky of *Migration*. A professional flutist, Mary Jo was drawn to quilting because "Unlike music in which you can never take back a note once it's been played wrong, in quilting, if you don't like it, you can go back and change it." Collection of Mary Jo Dalrymple.

37. *Descending*
A small quilt pieced from squares and quarter-circle-in-the-square blocks. A combination of American calico, tie-dyed fabric by Jennifer Brooke, and scraps of Japanese *yukata* cloth. Designing and piecing by Pepper Cory; quilting by Gail Hill.

38. *Fuego en la Noche (Fire in the Night)*
This modern masterpiece by self-taught quiltmaker Barbara Oliver Hartman combines quarter-circle units with other geometric shapes, some pieced, others hand-painted on the quilt's surface. Citing Amish quilts, Art Deco architecture, and Navajo rugs as artistic influences, Barbara says, "I go where the quilt takes me." Collection of Barbara Oliver Hartman.

THE NO-CURVE DRUNKARD'S PATH

There are still unbelievers among you. Even after reading this far and perusing the step-by-step instructions of the previous chapter, some of you are not convinced that you will ever try a Drunkard's Path. But the Drunkard's Path needs no further promotion—it has already attracted your attention. Now you are perhaps muttering, "Isn't there some way I could piece a Drunkard's Path without curves?" The answer is yes.

There are at least four methods of piecing a Drunkard's Path without sewing curved seams. The first is an optical illusion that I call the Faux Drunkard's Path. It is the brainchild of quilt historian Barbara Brackman. Acting on a suggestion from Ruth MacDowell, Barbara devised a method that produces the effect of the perfect miniature Drunkard's Path blocks.

*Figure 28.
The Faux
Drunkard's Path.*

THE FAUX DRUNKARD'S PATH

Essentially, the Faux Drunkard's Path (Figure 28) requires that you locate the right fabrics. These need to be two fabrics in fairly large-scale polka dots. One fabric should be a dark polka dot on light, such as red dots on white, and the other a light polka dot on dark, such as white dots on red. The dots must be the same size—take your ruler when you go fabric shopping!

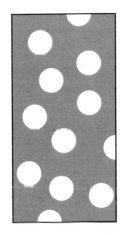
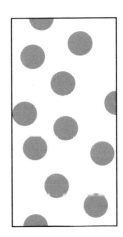

1) Measure the dots on both fabrics to ensure they are indeed the same size. The colors of the polka dots should be the same (for example, white-on-red and red-on-white).

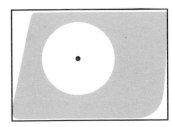

2) Locate the exact center of the dot.

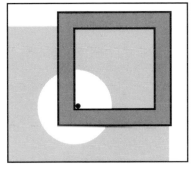

3) Place a window template over the dot with the lower left corner of the inside window corresponding to the dot's center. Trace around the template and cut out the square.

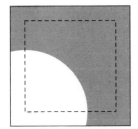

4) The quarter-circle, when viewed in the square (which has its ¼" seam allowance), will appear to be more than a quarter-circle until the squares are sewn together.

5) Cut out eight of the white dot on dark background. Cut out eight of the dark dot on white background.

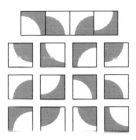

6) Assemble the squares as you normally would for a Drunkard's Path block.

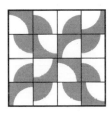

7) Without close examination, no one will be able to tell you haven't pieced a miniature Drunkard's Path.

Prepare the fabrics as you would for any other quilting project (wash, dry, iron). Next make a small window template. Commercially made window templates are usually fabricated from metal. You can make your own from sturdy plastic or posterboard. The inside window of the template should be large enough so that when an inside corner is placed on the middle point of a dot on the fabric, it frames a quarter-dot and simulates a Drunkard's Path curve. Move the window template around over the dots to frame the "Drunkard's Path" squares, trace around the outside of the template, and cut out the squares using scissors.

Cut eight squares from the light-on-dark dot and eight squares from the dark-on-light dot. Arrange the squares as you would a Drunkard's Path block and sew together in rows. The effect is stunning. If you quilt this little eye-fooler, no one will be able to tell (without close examination) that the fabrics were printed (see Photo 31).

The only drawback to such selective cutting is that it produces Swiss cheese holes all through your fabric. Depending on the placement of the polka dots, you can quickly go through a lot of material. My miniature Faux Drunkard's Path quilt (8" square without borders) took a quarter-yard of each of the polka-dot fabrics I used.

QUICK TOP-STITCHED DRUNKARD'S PATH

Method number two is the Quick Top-Stitched Drunkard's Path. (See Figure 29.) For a block, you will need a quarter-yard each of two contrasting fabrics. Look in the "Templates" section at the back of this book and use a *B* template in a 4" size. With the *B* template, cut eight pieces from the dark fabric and eight from the light. You will not use the matching *A* template. Do not mark pinning dots, seams, or clip the curves.

Since the top stitching will show on all the pieces, you must decide whether you want the stitching to show by using a contrasting color of thread (for decoration) or if you prefer the stitches to blend with the colors of the fabrics of the block. If the latter, before stitching, experiment with the most harmonious thread color by draping threads of several colors across both pieces. The thread that shows the least on both colors will be your best choice for a blending thread. Of course, you may match thread colors exactly and switch threads as you sew the pieces. That's more work. In order to stand up and declare you are the master of this top-stitching method, try piecing a Drunkard's Path in holiday red and green. Do the top stitching in metallic gold thread. The effect can be quite lovely.

The edge stitcher foot which must be used on your machine to do this method may look different from machine to machine. This attachment isn't very popular today, since it is best suited for small tucks and fancy top-stitching—both sewing techniques that are somewhat out of fashion. But if you have an older machine, it's worthwhile getting out those antique stitching attachments and experimenting with them.

I came upon this method by examining an old quilt top, made around 1910 (see Photo 32). Obviously pieced by a seamstress who sewed a lot and was familiar with her sewing machine, the stitching on top was a clever and timesaving way to sew the curves of the Drunkard's Path. Using that anonymous quilter's ingenious method, I made a Drunkard's Path block in about an hour.

Figure 29. The Quick Top-Stitched Drunkard's Path.

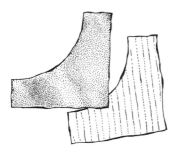

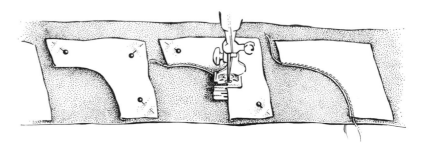

1) Using the wing-shape (Template *B*), cut eight from each color fabric. Do not mark pinning dots or clip the curves. The *A* template (quarter-circle) is not used at all.

4) Pin the pieces (right side up) to strips of their opposite color fabric.

5) Using the edge stitcher foot on your machine, feed the pieces through the machine.

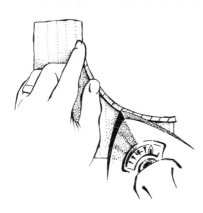

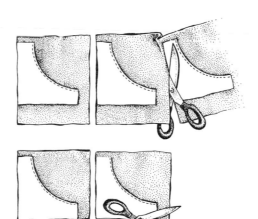

2) Take the pieces to the ironing board. Turn them wrong side up. Run your index finger up the curved edge of each, rolling the edge like a scarf hem. Follow (at a safe distance) with an iron set on "Cotton."

6) Cut apart the blocks along the perpendicular sides of the *B* shapes.

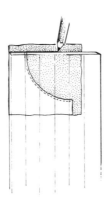

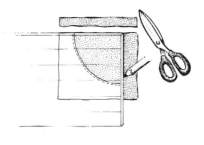

7) With a quilt ruler, square off the extra fabric at the ruler's corner, and cut out the pieces. Trim fabric from the block's back.

3) Press all sixteen pieces on the wrong side, then turn them over. The edge is pressed down about ⅛".

8) A finished quick top-stitched Drunkard's Path block.

THE LOG CABIN DRUNKARD'S PATH

This is a simple straight-seam patchwork pattern. While it is properly a Log Cabin variation, when the blocks are arranged to mimic the rhythm of a Drunkard's Path, it assumes the meandering quality of the curved pattern (Figure 30). You will need a half-yard piece of two different fabrics.

Figure 30.
The Log Cabin
Drunkard's Path.

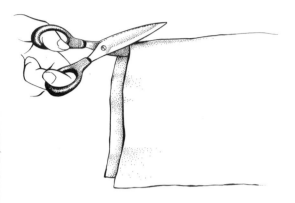

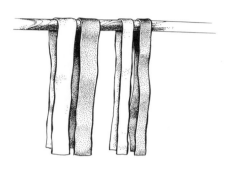

1) Cut the half-yard pieces of both fabrics in two pieces. From one piece, cut 2" wide strips. From the other, cut 1¼" strips. Repeat for the second fabric.

2) Keep the strips straight by hanging them apart on a dowel.

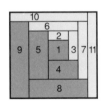

3) Piece the blocks in the order indicated. Make eight blocks of each type.

Log Cabin Drunkard's Path Quilt. The "curves" of the blocks imitate the curves of the Drunkard's Path block.

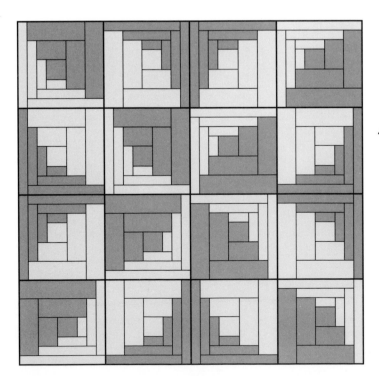

4) After assembling sixteen of the blocks, sew them together following the diagram.

Divide the half-yard pieces at the fold and cut them in half (the pieces will be about 18" x 22"). You will have two dark pieces and two light pieces. From one dark and one light piece, cut 2" wide strips. From the remaining dark and light pieces, cut strips 1¼" wide. You'll have stacks of strips from both widths (2" and 1¼"), from both the dark and light fabrics.

To assemble the Log Cabin blocks, refer to Step #3 in Figure 30. The thinner strips (1¼" wide) will represent the wing shape (the *B*) of the Drunkard's Path. The wider strips (2") will be the quarter-circle (the *A* part). Unlike the classic Log Cabin, this variation does not use a different color, such as red, at its center. The little square that starts the piecing of the block is not at the exact center of the pattern but becomes the "bulge" of the mock curve.

Rather than make individual templates for this block, I assemble the pattern as I do any Log Cabin. I start with the little square, sew strips to it in order, and cut to fit.

The only drawback to the Log Cabin Drunkard's Path is that each unit comes out 6½" square. With that large a unit, the pattern is suited to a single "block" wallhanging or a very large quilt. Of course, the final size of the block can be changed if the size of the strips is likewise adjusted. The formula is to work with strips that divide into two groups. When the seam allowances of these strips are sewn, the "logs" will be ¾" and 1½" wide— one exactly twice as wide as the other.

THE LAST METHOD

One other patchwork pattern that impersonates the Drunkard's Path is a modern straight-seam block called Lightning (Figure 31). Its designer, Beth Gutcheon, stated that while she admired the Drunkard's Path, she was not about to sew all those curves. So she invented Lightning which indeed does capture the feeling of the Drunkard's Path but without curved seams. Look closely at the illustration and you'll see what I mean.

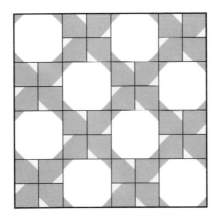

Figure 31.
The pattern Lightning by Beth Gutcheon.

Now that you have read this chapter, you have no good reason *not* to try the Drunkard's Path pattern. From trompe d'oeil (Faux Drunkard's Path) to new stitching tricks (the Top-Stitched Drunkard's Path) to the straight-seam impersonators (Log Cabin Drunkard's Path and Lightning), there are at least four ways to get around the curve problem of the traditional Drunkard's Path. And who knows? Perhaps after a success with one of these methods, you will feel confident enough to try the curves of a real Drunkard's Path. C'mon! Bend a little!

CONCLUSION

Every famous musician will admit he or she had to practice scales when first learning music. Artists often make many preliminary sketches before any paint is committed to the canvas. Likewise, quiltmakers—if they want to be proficient at their craft—must practice and hone their skills.

In this heyday of quick-cutting tools, strip piecing shortcuts, and timesaving tips, a great deal of emphasis has been placed on straight-seam quilt piecing. I know some really good (and famous) quilters who have never attempted a curved seam. Enter the humble Drunkard's Path pattern.

The Drunkard's Path is far and away the best patchwork pattern on which to learn, and practice, sewing the curved seam. That the Drunkard's Path is also an absorbing design challenge that expands the quiltmaker's creativity is the icing on the cake—an unexpected bonus for having chosen this old-time patchwork favorite.

Although I have been piecing Drunkard's Path quilts for years, my efforts will not cease with the writing of this book. Having gone public with my fascination for the pattern, my hope is that many more quiltmakers, like yourself, will accompany me further in the adventure of curved seam piecing.

Once you have made your first Drunkard's Path sample, you may get a little cocky. Curved seams will simply be no big deal any more. Like the pianist who labors over exercises and then finds that all the melodies flow more smoothly, so you will find that other, more complex curved patterns are within your grasp. The Drunkard's Path pattern is your entree to truly creative quilt designing. No longer are you obliged to only follow the straight and narrow style of quiltmaking. New paths are calling you and it's time to saddle up and ride...many Happy Trails to you!

The author, age 5, astride a penny-ride horse. Wichita, Kansas, 1956.

PATTERN INDEX FOR DRUNKARD'S PATH
AND VARIATIONS

How to use: Look at the drawings of the blocks. There may be several renditions of the same block since different placement of lights and darks within the block "disguises" the piecing. Below the drawing(s) are that block's names. The most popular name (that is, the name most commonly used) is listed first. Next come alternate names. The final names are seldom used or used only by a particular group (such as the Amish) or come from an individual source (such as Shogren's *Compendium*). This index is meant as a guide, not as the final authority on the subject of Drunkard's Path possibilities and their names.

Drunkard's Path, Rob Peter to Pay Paul, Rocky Road to Dublin, Drunkard's Trail, Solomon's Puzzle, Old Maid's Puzzle, Wanderer in the Wilderness (Canada), Wonder of the World, Endless Trail, Crooked Path, Boston Trail, Country Cousin, Old Maid's Dilemma (Iowa Amish), Rocky Road to Durbin's (Kentucky), The Milkmaid's Path (Virginia), The Drunken Herald (England)

Rocky Road to Dublin, The Road to California, Oregon Trail, Country Husband, Pumpkin Vine

Wonder of the World, Fool's Puzzle, Solomon's Puzzle, Old Maid's Puzzle, Wish-U-Well (Wish You Well, I Wish You Well), Tumbleweed, Whirlpool, Arkansas Troubles

Drunkard's Path (alternate block)

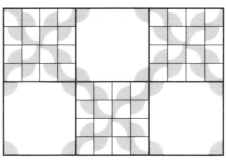

Drunkard's Path (Carlie Sexton pattern, from the 1930s)

Drunkard's Path, Fool's Puzzle, Wonder of the World, Algonquin Trail, Algonquin Path

Falling Timbers

Mill Wheel,   Sunshine and
Steeplechase,   Shadows
Rob Peter to Pay Paul

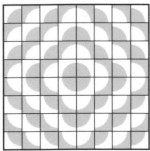

Love Ring, Lone Ring, Sun Dance (in shades of yellow and gold), Nonesuch, Rippling Waters, Trip Around the World (Canadian Mennonite), Ocean Waves (Amish), Jig Saw Puzzle, Ozark Puzzle

Reflections of Love

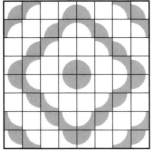

Moorish Design

Illinois Rose

Chain Links

Snake Trail, Falling Timbers, Diagonal Stripes, Vine of Friendship, Chain

Dove

The Dove

Doves

Bird

Cleopatra's Puzzle

King's Tut's Crown

Note: These blocks are technically the same.

Ghost Walk, Anna Dancing

Baby Bunting

Indiana Puzzle, Mill Wheel, Rob Peter to Pay Paul

Tumbling Circles

Jockey Cap

Indiana Puzzle, Snowball

Harlequin

Old Mill Wheel

Snowball

Snowball, Polka Dots

Snowball

Harvest Moon

Around the World

Dirty Windows

Snowy Windows

Drunkard's Patchwork

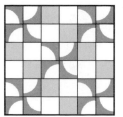

Indian Path, Indian Patch

Drunkard's Garden

Quilter's Delight,
Crazy Quilt

Turtle on a Quilt,
Terrapin

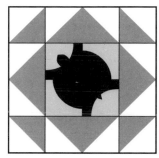

Turtle in a Puddle

The Road Home

Aunt Polly's Puzzle

Owl   Kitty   Butterfly

(Details embroidered or appliquéd)

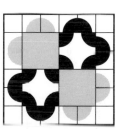

Around the Mountain

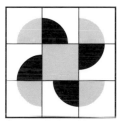

Opening Valentines

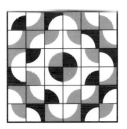

Devil's Puzzle

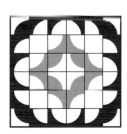

Kathy Sue's Puzzle

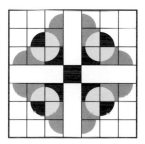

Curved Nouveau

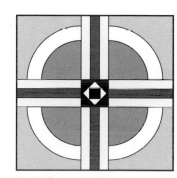

Toll House and
Plank Road

Pictures in the Stairwell

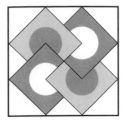

Puzzle Boxes

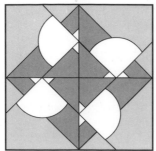

Scallop Shells

String Quilt in a Sea Shell

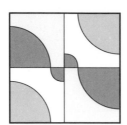

Ida's Friendship Block

Snake's Trail,
Drunkard's Trail,
Snake in the Hollow
(when arranged in a
maze setting)

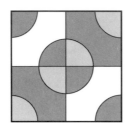

Bow and Arrows,
Marble Quilt,
Steeplechase,
Boston Puzzle,
Pullman Puzzle

Lollipop Trees

Anvils

Bridges

Wind Chimes

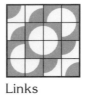

Mushrooms

Whirling Mushrooms

Links

Mirage

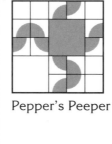

Throwing Star

Whirling Arches

Pepper's Peeper

Mystery Pattern (overall set)

58

TEMPLATES

All templates shown here include ¼" seam allowances. The solid lines are the actual size of the templates and represent the sewing lines. The dots designate pinning holes. The templates are cut out along the dashed lines.

Most of the blocks in the Pattern Index are formed by combining coordinating *A* and *B* templates. *A* is the quarter-circle shape, and *B* is the L-shaped remainder. Some blocks require squares as well. For example, a classic Drunkard's Path block in a 12" size would require the 3" *A* and the 3" *B* templates. But a block such as Kathy Sue's Puzzle using 3" *A* and 3" *B* templates also needs a 3" square. The Kathy Sue's Puzzle block made would then measure 18" since that pattern is based on a six-by-six grid.

To choose templates, look through *Happy Trails* and see which quilts attract you. Notice the grid that the individual block is based on (four-by-four, five-by-five, etc.). Decide the size block you want to work on, then find the corresponding templates here. If you insist on working in a size block *not* found in these templates, refer to Chapter 2 for drawing instructions.

Most of the familiar Drunkard's Path blocks are formed from these *A* and *B* templates.

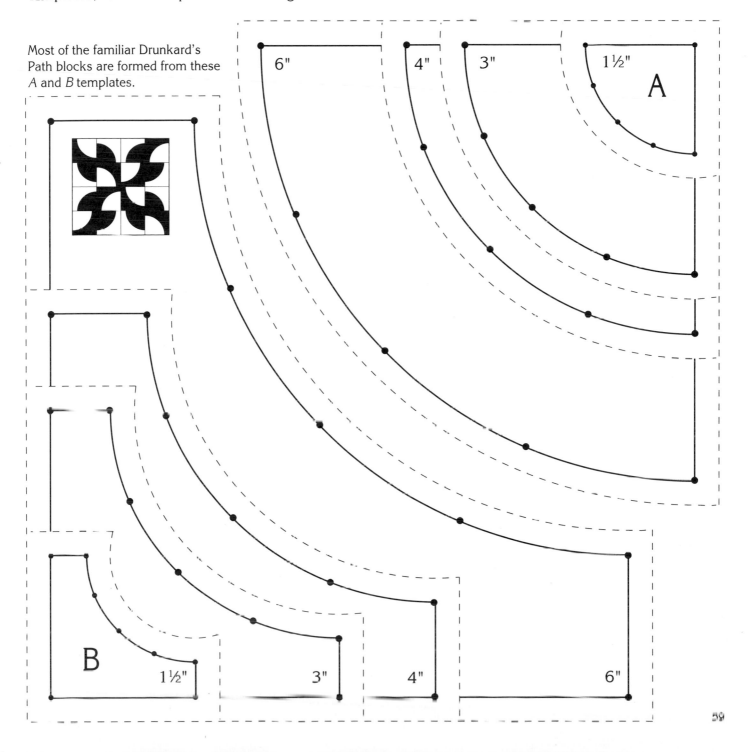

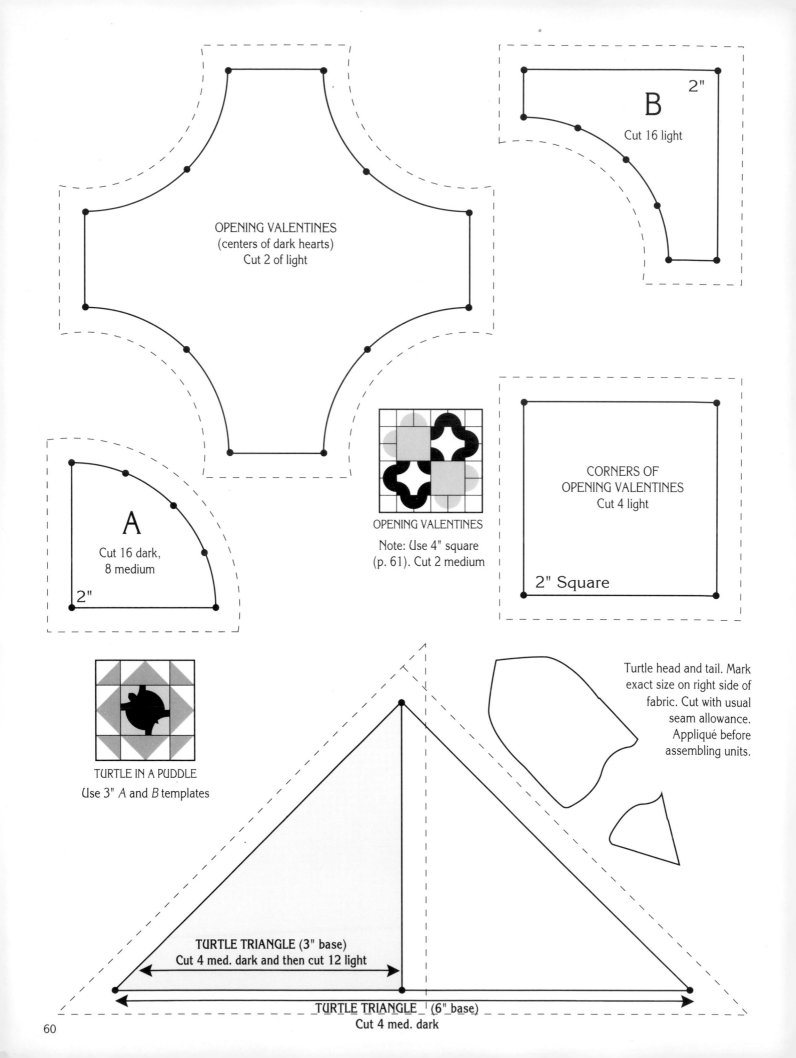

OPENING VALENTINES
(centers of dark hearts)
Cut 2 of light

B
2"
Cut 16 light

A
Cut 16 dark,
8 medium
2"

OPENING VALENTINES
Note: Use 4" square
(p. 61). Cut 2 medium

CORNERS OF
OPENING VALENTINES
Cut 4 light
2" Square

TURTLE IN A PUDDLE
Use 3" A and B templates

Turtle head and tail. Mark
exact size on right side of
fabric. Cut with usual
seam allowance.
Appliqué before
assembling units.

TURTLE TRIANGLE (3" base)
Cut 4 med. dark and then cut 12 light

TURTLE TRIANGLE (6" base)
Cut 4 med. dark

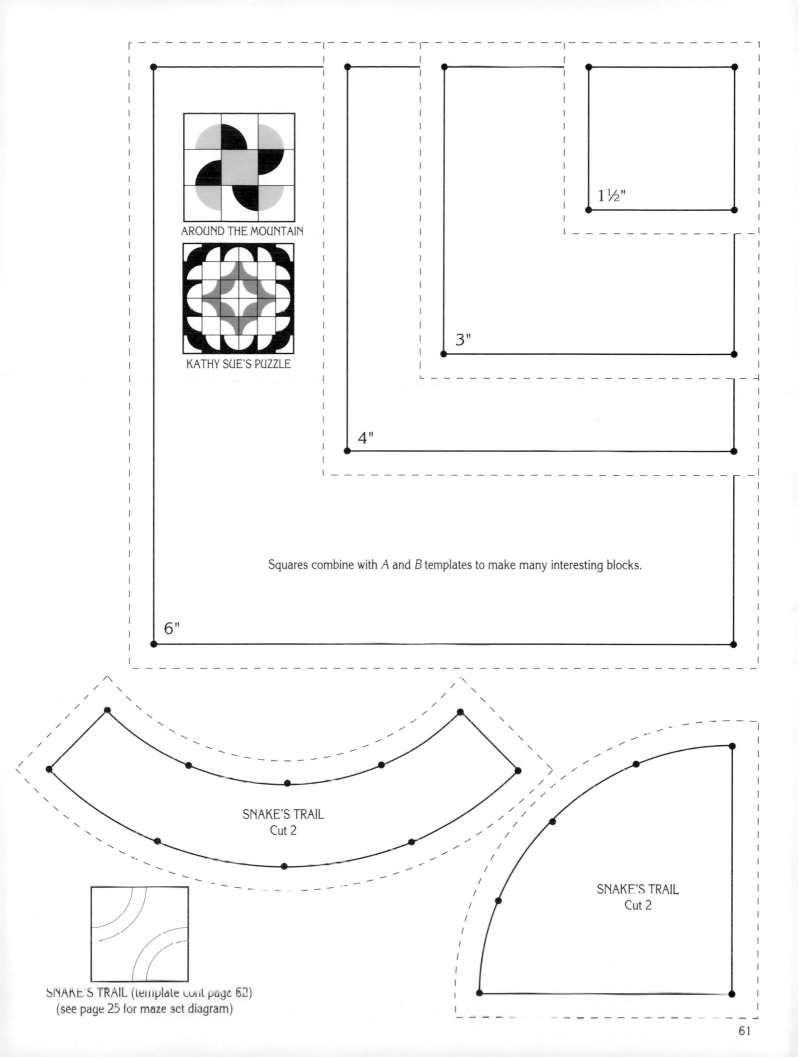

AROUND THE MOUNTAIN

KATHY SUE'S PUZZLE

1½"

3"

4"

6"

Squares combine with *A* and *B* templates to make many interesting blocks.

SNAKE'S TRAIL
Cut 2

SNAKE'S TRAIL
Cut 2

SNAKE'S TRAIL (template cont page 62)
(see page 25 for maze set diagram)

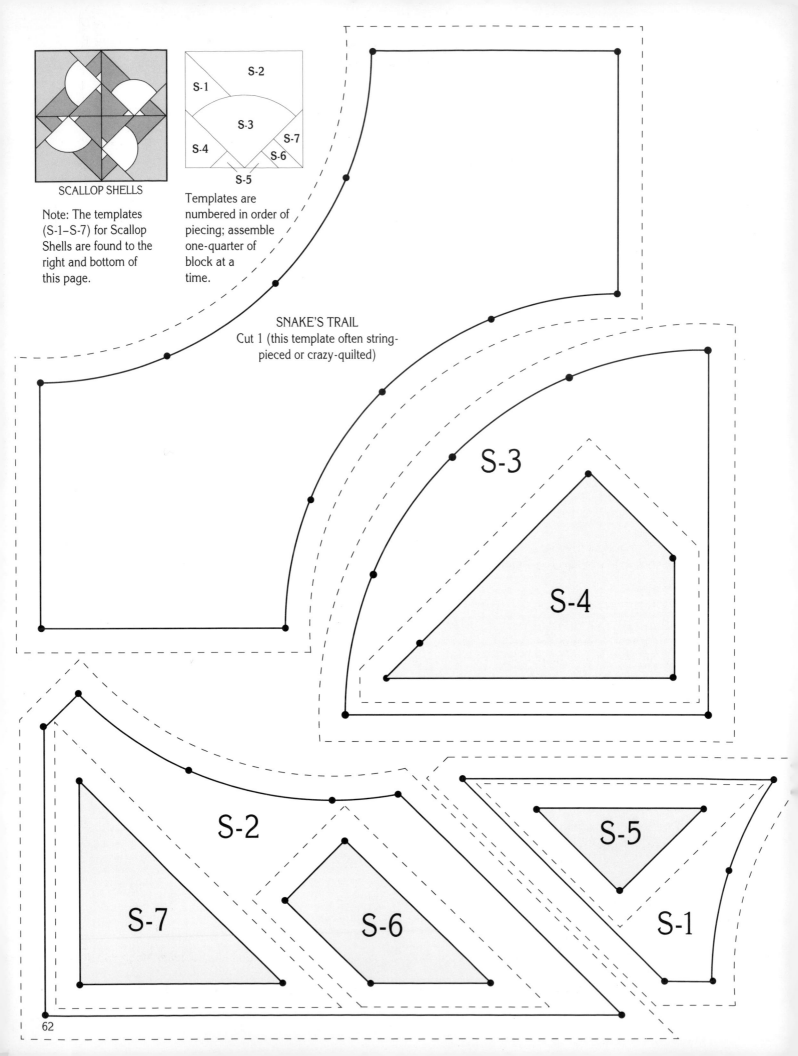

SCALLOP SHELLS

Note: The templates (S-1–S-7) for Scallop Shells are found to the right and bottom of this page.

S-2
S-1
S-3
S-4
S-7
S-6
S-5

Templates are numbered in order of piecing; assemble one-quarter of block at a time.

SNAKE'S TRAIL
Cut 1 (this template often string-pieced or crazy-quilted)

S-3

S-4

S-2

S-7

S-6

S-5

S-1

BIBLIOGRAPHY

Some of these books may be hard to find. Check your public library or the libraries of longtime quiltmakers. An "R" at the end of an entry means the book has research material on the Drunkard's Path pattern. A "T" means the book has technical information. Books without an "R" or "T" contain general information.

Anderson, Mary Lou. *Precision Machine Piecing of Curved Seams*. Nashville, Tennessee: Stitch 'n String, 1988. (T)

Betterton, Shiela. *The American Quilt Tradition*. London, England: The American Museum in Britain, 1976.

Beyer, Jinny. *The Quilter's Album of Blocks and Borders*. McLean, Virginia: EPM Publications, 1980. (R)

Boyink, Betty. *Michigan Quilters and Their Designs*. Grand Haven, Michigan: Betty Boyink Publishing, 1983.

Brackman, Barbara. "Drunkard's Path: Polka-Dot Shortcut." *Quilter's Newsletter Magazine*, January 1989, p. 48. (T)

———. *An Encyclopedia of Pieced Quilt Patterns*. Lawrence, Kansas: Prairie Flower Publishing, 1984. (R)

———. "New York Patterns." *Quilter's Newsletter Magazine*, May 1984, pp. 26-27.

———. "Oklahoma Pattern Collection." *Quilter's Newsletter Magazine*, May 1985, pp. 9-12.

Buettner, Cynthia. *Patchwork Parade*. Published by the author, 1983.

Carter, Hazel. *Virginia Quilts*. Vienna, Virginia: The Continental Quilting Congress, 1987.

Clarke, Mary Washington. *Kentucky Quilts and Their Makers*. Lexington, Kentucky: University of Kentucky Press, 1976.

Colby, Averil. *Patchwork*. London, England: B. T. Batsford, Ltd., 1978.

Conroy, Mary. *300 Years of Canada's Quilts*. Toronto: Griffin House, 1976.

Cory, Pepper. *Crosspatch: Inspirations in Multi-Block Quilts*. Lafayette, California: C&T Publishing, 1989. (T)

Dubois, Jean. *The Wool Quilt*. Durango, Colorado: La Plata Press, 1978.

Duke, Dennis, and Harding, Deborah. *America's Glorious Quilts*. New York: Macmillan, 1987.

Finley, Ruth. *Old Patchwork Quilts*. Newton Centre, Massachusetts: Charles T. Branford Company, 1970.

"Great American Classics: Drunkard's Path & Variations." *Quilter's Newsletter Magazine*, July/August 1978, pp. 9-12. (R and T)

Gutcheon, Beth, and Gutcheon, Jeffrey. *The Quilt Design Workbook*. New York: Rawson Associates Publishers, 1976.

Halgrimson, Jan. *Great Scrap Bag Quilts*. Edmonds, Washington: Weaver-Finch Publications, 1980.

Holstein, Jonathan. *The Pieced Quilt*. New York: Gallahad Books, 1973.

Houck, Carter, and Miller, Myron. *American Quilts and How to Make Them*. New York: Scribner's, 1975.

James, Michael. *The Second Quiltmaker's Handbook*. Englewood Cliffs, New Jersey: Prentice-Hall, 1981. (T)

Kaether, Marjorie, and Shantz, Susan B. *Quilts of Waterloo County*. Waterloo, Ontario: Johanns Graphics, 1990.

The Kansas City Star Quilt Pattern Collection. Oklahoma City, Oklahoma: Central Oklahoma Quilters Guild, 1989. (R)

Khin, Yvonne M. *The Collector's Dictionary of Quilt Names and Patterns*. Washington, D.C.: Acropolis Books, Ltd., 1980. (R)

Kramer, Monta Lea. *New Path*. Parsons, Tennessee: Lamb Art Press, 1989. (T)

Martin, Judy. *Scrap Quilts*. Wheatridge, Colorado: Moon Over the Mountain Publishing, 1985.

Murphy, Anita. *Drunkard's Path*. San Marcos, California: American School of Needlework, Inc., Publishing, 1991.

Oklahoma Quilt Heritage Project. *Oklahoma Heritage Quilts*. Paducah, Kentucky: American Quilter's Society, 1990.

Orbelo, Beverly Ann. *A Texas Quilting Primer*. San Antonio, Texas: Corona Publishing, 1980.

Orlofsky, Patsy, and Orlofsky, Myron. *Quilts in America*. New York: McGraw-Hill, 1974.

Pellman, Rachel, and Pellman, Kenneth. *The World of Amish Quilts*. Intercourse, Pennsylvania: Good Books, 1984.

"Piecing Curved Seams." *Quilter's Newsletter Magazine*, October 1980, pp. 13-14. (T)

Rae, Janet. *The Quilts of the British Isles*. New York: Dutton, 1987.

Reddick, Mary. "One Simple Pattern." *Quilt Almanac* (Vol. 8, No. 1, 1989), pp. 24-25. (T)

Remel, Judy. *The Quilt I.D. Book*. New York: Prentice-Hall, 1986. (R)

Robertson, Elizabeth Wells. *American Quilts*. New York: The Studio Publications, 1948.

Sexton, Carlie. *Quaint Quilts*. Des Moines, Iowa, n.d.

Shirer, Marie. "The Great American Quilt Classics: Drunkard's Path Revisited." *Quilter's Newsletter Magazine*, May 1989, pp. 34-37. (T and R)

Shogren, Linda. *The Drunkard's Path Compendium*. San Mateo, California: Pieceful Pleasures, 1978. (R)

RESORCES

➤ BOOKS

All quilting books currently in print are available through Quilting Books Unlimited, 1911 West Wilson Street, Batavia, IL 60510. Send $1 for a catalog.

➤ FABRICS

Fabric swatches (over 350) and a catalog of quilting supplies are available for $5 from Cotton Patch Mail Order, 1025 Brown Avenue, Lafayette, CA 94549.

➤ PATTERNS

Bird, Butterfly, Curved Nouveau, Kitty, Owl, Reflections of Love, and Tumbling Circles are from the book *Drunkard's Path* by Anita Murphy. Inquire at your local quilt shop or write American School of Needlework, Inc., Publishing, 1455 Linda Vista Drive, San Marcos, CA 92069.

Around the Mountain is available from Feathered Star Productions, 2151 7th Avenue West, Seattle, WA 98119. Send $1 plus a legal-size stamped self-addressed envelope for the pattern.

Lightning is found in *The Quilt Design Workbook* by Beth and Jeffrey Gutcheon. Since this book is not presently in print, try your public library.

Mirage (and other quarter-circle patterns) are found in the booklet *Patchwork Parade* by Cynthia Buettner. Send $8 plus $2 shipping to Strings Attached, 5250 Norfolk, Lima, OH 45806.

Puzzle Boxes is from the book *Great Scrap Bag Quilts* by Jan Halgrimson. Send $11.95 plus $1.75 shipping to Weaver-Finch Publications, P.O. Box 353, Edmonds, WA 98020.

Toll House and Plank Road is from the book *Michigan Quilters and Their Designs* by Betty Boyink. Send $10 plus $2 shipping to Betty Boyink Publishing, 818 Sheldon Road, Grand Haven, MI 49417.

➤ TOOLS

Acrylic templates for rotary cutting Drunkard's Path and the Multi-View Lens are from Quilter's Rule™. If your local quilt shop does not have them, a mail-order source is Our Southern Heritage, P.O. Box 2340, Silver Springs, FL 32688.

The hand punch to make ⅛" holes in templates is available from United Art and Educational Supply Company, 3736 Wells Street, Indianapolis, IN 46855. Ask for Hand Punch #MCK-401R. The price is $5 postpaid.

Many sizes of window templates are available in Ardco™ Templates from QuiltSmith, 252 Cedar Road, Poquoson, VA 23662.

Other C&T titles by Pepper Cory:

Quilting Designs from the Amish
Quilting Designs from Antique Quilts
Crosspatch: Inspirations in Multi-Block Quilts

For a complete listing of fine quilting books from C&T Publishing, write for a free catalog:
C&T Publishing
P.O. Box 1456
Lafayette, CA 94549